The paths of Buddhism

the silk road zen Mandala
tolerance Siddharta
The Lesser Vehicle
nirvana The Dalai Lama

Jean-Luc Toula-Breysse

CASSELL&CO

8

is the number of auspicious signs in Tibetan culture.

▶ 80

'If the **Six Flavours** are not in harmony and the **Three Virtues** are lacking, then the Tenzo [head cook] is not really serving the community.' ▶ 112

Tenzin Gyatso, the 14th Dalai Lama
In 1940 : *he ascended the Lion Throne at the age of five, becoming the official spiritual and secular leader of the Tibetans. He was 13 years old when Chinese Communist troops invaded his country.*
He went into exile 17 March 1959.
In 1989, *he received the Nobel Peace Prize.*

 98

2,500 years ago

the Buddha was a mortal man searching for the ultimate truth. He taught that the path of deliverance from the endless cycle of life–death–rebirth could be found through deep meditation. ▶ 15

The 5 buddhas of meditation

Vairocana, the Radiating One
Aksobhya, the Steadfast One
Ratnasambhava, the Jewel-Born One
Amithaba, the Boundless Light
Amoghasiddhi, the All-Accomplishing One

The Lesser Vehicle

or Hinayana, has spread throughout Sri Lanka, Myanmar, Thailand, Cambodia, Laos and South Vietnam.

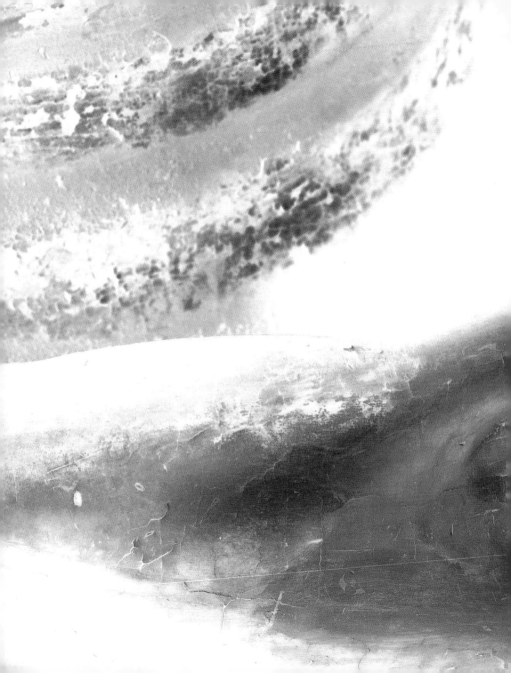

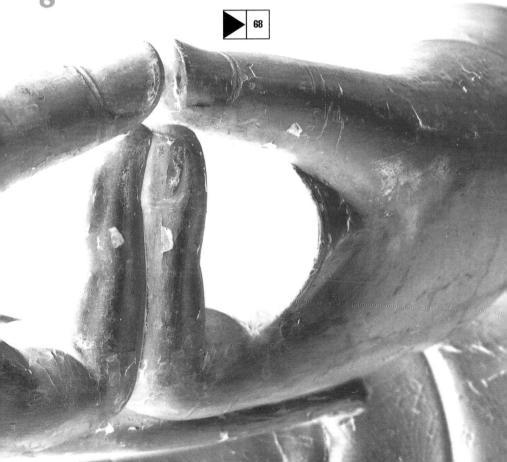

Reasoning, embracing, offering, giving, meditation...

These sacred ideas and beliefs are represented by **the different gestures of the Buddhas' hands.**

▶ 68

Unlike the great monotheistic traditions (Judaism, Christianity and Islam),
Buddhism does not refer to a divine revelation.

To collect the
Buddhist scriptures,
Xuanzang,
**the most famous Chinese
pilgrim**,
was said to have confronted
1,000 dangers as he travelled along the
Silk Road.

▶ 63

1814

Sir Stamford Raffles discovered **Borobudur**, in central Java. This supreme example of Buddhist art, aligned according to **the 4 cardinal points**, stands as a symbol of the earth and sky. The monumental crowning **stupa** is supported by 72 smaller stupas, each of which houses its own stone buddha.

▶ 71

The first of the Four Noble Truths

teaches that we are all subject to suffering, the second tells us the cause of that suffering, the third teaches that the suffering can be ended, and the fourth shows us the path to its cessation.

 25

'When the mind is still, the floor where I sit is endless space.'

Muso Soseki

Because the Japanese Zen garden has been designed to promote contemplation, no paths are permitted to cross its surface.

The sand and rocks symbolise the 'void-ness' at the heart of Zen Buddhism.

 78

Z̲Everything is
Zen

beginning with the landscape itself.

DISCOVER

THE MAJOR EVENTS IN THE LIFE OF THE HISTORICAL BUDDHA,
SIDDHARTA GAUTAMA. HIS TEACHINGS AND THE BUDDHIST DOCTRINE.
THE FOUR NOBLE TRUTHS. THE THREE MAIN BUDDHIST SCHOOLS.
HOW BUDDHISM SWEPT ACROSS ASIA, DEVELOPING AND
BLOSSOMING INTO ONE OF THE WORLD'S THREE GREAT RELIGIONS.

The historical Buddha was born in the fifth century BC, in Northern India. However, beyond this bald fact, much remains uncertain and even mythical, including the chronicles describing the Buddha's life and teachings. According to Buddhist tradition, he was born a prince of the Sakya clan and was given the personal name Siddharta Gautama (Siddharta means 'one whose purpose has been accomplished'). But, in truth, as will be seen later in this book, 'Buddha' is a title rather than a name, and is accorded to someone who has achieved something remarkable. 'Buddha' literally means 'awakened one', someone who has 'woken up' to the way things really are and has understood their true nature.

Although Siddharta was born into a privileged lifestyle, he gradually became disillusioned with material things. When confronted with the existential realities of old age, sickness and death, he had a desire to understand the origin of human suffering and whether it was possible to achieve liberation from it. Siddharta left his princely home and all its luxuries, vowing to find a release from suffering. In his quest for the truth, he spent a number of years as a wandering ascetic, practising yogic austerities. Nevertheless, he remained dissatisfied, and eventually abandoned this lifestyle. Finally, on the banks of the Nairanyjana River, while seated in meditation beneath a fig tree, he underwent an experience so profound that he believed he had come to the end of his quest. From this moment Siddharta had become an 'awakened one', a Buddha. He had been awakened to suffering, its cause, its cessation, and the path leading to its cessation.

BUDDHA AND CHILD
The serenity of this stone buddha holds a hypnotic power over the child. (Caves of Yun-Kan, China, fifth century.)

During his 45 years of teaching, the Buddha stressed that he taught only two things: 'suffering and the cessation of suffering.' Anything that did not relate directly to this task was seen as irrelevant and mere philosophical speculation. Thus, throughout its history, Buddhism has avoided the question of God, regarding the concept as unrelated to emancipation from suffering. According to Buddhist scriptures, when the Buddha was asked whether God existed, he simply remained silent, refusing to be drawn into speculation. All schools of Buddhism emphasise that liberation from suffering is the task of the individual, and that one cannot expect help from a God or even from a Buddha. The path that the Buddha teaches is a moral one, and is directed towards eradicating actions founded on greed, hatred and delusion. Instead, our actions in the world are to be based on generosity, compassion, and wisdom. The Buddhist path is therefore a path of mental transformation – a way of transforming minds steeped in greed, hatred and delusion into minds permeated by generosity, compassion and wisdom.

Buddhism has generated numerous movements, schools and practices throughout the world, from India to Japan and China to South-East Asia, and has been established in the West since the late 19th century. The spread of Buddhism throughout Eurasia, together with its ability to coexist with local beliefs, such as ancestor worship and Taoism in China, shamanism in

Mongolia and Korea, the Bon religion in Tibet and Shinto rites in Japan, testify to its accessibility. The various forms of Buddhism that have emerged within native cultures all share one fundamental belief – that suffering is to be overcome.

THE NATURE OF THE BUDDHIST TEXTS

The original teaching of the Buddha is available to us only through the ancient texts, which were set down in writing some four centuries after his death. These texts already reflect the divergence that existed between the various sects. Moreover, only a small proportion of the original literature has survived – either in the Indian original, or in Chinese or Tibetan translations. For at least four centuries, the Buddha's teaching was preserved solely by oral transmission, and very probably in different, though related, dialects. This, and the absence of an authoritative religious hierarchy, constitute two obvious sources of distortion and alteration of the original message. For these reasons, our knowledge of the doctrine actually taught by the Buddha himself remains somewhat vague and conjectural.

INDIAN SOCIETY AT THE TIME OF THE BUDDHA

By the sixth century BC, Indian society was already organised into a rigid class system (*varōa*). The Brahmin, the elite priestly caste, wielded immense religious power, making it difficult for ordinary people to challenge the authority of the priests. Members of the lowest caste were completely excluded from participating in religious rituals, because of their perceived lowly status. Numerous new sects and schools of thought began to emerge as a direct reaction to the Brahmin's stranglehold on organised religion, and so it was into a complex and pluralistic religious world that the Buddha was born.

BIRTH OF THE BUDDHA

This Indian painting depicts the birth of the Buddha. His mother, Queen Maya – in the foreground – died shortly afterwards.

The earlier Buddhist texts were not biographical, as their purpose was simply to pass on the Buddha's teachings. Even the exact dates of the Buddha's life, birth and death remain uncertain, and there are vast discrepancies between the dates offered by contemporary scholarship and those offered by the various traditions of Buddhism. The most widely quoted dates for the life of the Buddha are 566–486 BC. However, modern scholars such as Richard Gombrich tend to place the death of the Buddha much closer to 400 BC rather than 500 BC. Of course, Buddhists might argue that historical details are of minor importance, as they would prefer to concentrate on the Master's religious teachings. Nevertheless, today's historians all acknowledge the existence of Gautama. His first name, Siddharta, means 'one whose purpose has been accomplished'. In Buddhist tradition, he is known by several other names: Sakyamuni (meaning Sage of the Sakya), the Blessed and the Master (by his disciples). The word Buddha itself means 'Awakened (or Enlightened) One'.

THE LIFE OF THE HISTORICAL BUDDHA

Siddharta Gautama was born in a small town in the foothills of the Nepalese Himalayas. According to the *Chronicles* of Ceylon he was born in 623 BC, but 20th-century chronological corrections give the date as 563 BC. He was the son of Suddhodana, the king or great chieftain of the Sakya tribe – providing the origin of the surname Sakyamuni – and of Queen Maya, who died shortly after his birth. Like all young boys of his age and rank, he received a noble education, including instruction in science, horsemanship and

archery. Even at an early age, the young prince showed signs of an unusual sensitivity. Once, when his father was performing a ritual ceremony, the boy, without any training, became absorbed in deep meditative concentration, which would later be called the First Meditation (or *dhyana*).

Despite these awakenings of his meditative nature, the prince continued to live a life of luxury and ease. At the age of 16 he was married to Princess Yasodhara, who later gave birth to a son. But, when Siddharta ventured outside his luxurious palace, he encountered human misery. Four encounters are said to have transformed his outlook on life, making him aware of suffering as the inescapable expression of the human condition. According to Buddhist legend, he first came across an old man, who caused him to realise that although old age is unwelcome it is inevitable. Later, he saw a cripple, and reflected that although people wish to avoid contact with sick people, illness is unavoidable. When saw a corpse, he realised that although people hate death it is the inevitable end of all. Finally, when he came across an ascetic, he was impressed by the man's serenity, and reflected that it was possible to renounce worldly things and be free from the entanglements of life. These disturbing episodes convinced the young prince that the affairs of the world and material pleasures could not satisfy him. He resolved to become a mendicant and practice asceticism. At the age of 29, despite his father's opposition, he renounced the members of his caste for life and left his luxurious family home. He withdrew from society, living on its margins and associating only with religious masters. Like many of his religious contemporaries, he sought to escape the suffering of existence. However, eventually he became dissatisfied with the teachings he had received, and resolved to continue his quest in his own way. In the company of five mendicants, Gautama subjected himself to the most severe asceticism, through self-mortification and fasting. But after inflicting a series of terrible trials and tribulations upon himself, he found that a life of deprivation was no better than a life of pleasure. He concluded that extreme asceticism was a mistake and that it represented pointless behaviour. It was this belief that later led him to preach sermons about the Middle Path, aiming at avoiding these two extremes – found as much in materialistic life as in asceticism.

Buddhist legend recounts that one night, after years of searching, while Siddharta was seated beneath a *pipal* tree near the Indian village of Bodhgaya, the demon Mara appeared, terrorising

him with the fear of death, in the form of an army, windstorms, sandstorms and whirlwinds. But Siddharta resisted and triumphed, overcoming all the challenges of the demon.

When Mara was vanquished, Siddharta attained the state of absolute awakening – a state in which he understood the truth, the cause, the cessation and the path to the cessation of suffering. From that moment he became an 'Awakened One', a Buddha, one who had attained Nirvana. The Buddha had quenched the fires of greed, hatred and delusion that kept human beings bound to the cycle of death and rebirth. From the moment of awakening, his actions would be motivated only by generosity, compassion and wisdom.

This account of Mara's temptation is seen as a parable of Siddharta's struggles to understand what binds us to existence. Pali tradition says that in the first part of that crucial night Siddharta acquired a supernatural ability to remember his past lives, and began to reflect on his past and how his lives had been directed by certain factors. Then, in the middle of the night, he saw how similar factors directed the lives of others, understanding how one's actions contribute to the course of life, and how things beyond one's control also influence it. He witnessed how greed, hatred, lust and confusion produced negative outcomes and realised that we should eliminate these, one by one, so as to increase our freedom and wisdom. At the end of the night, he had discovered the Four Noble Truths and became the Buddha. He called himself the Tathagata, 'One who has arrived', meaning that he had attained the truth.

Of course, we shall never know the true content of the Buddha's insights, but the differences between Buddhist philosophies hinge on the different interpretations of the events of that crucial night.

THE FIRST BUDDHIST MONKS

Seven days after achieving Enlightenment, Siddharta Gautama (henceforth the Buddha), continued his life of wandering. He decided to dedicate his life to explaining the Truth, the path that leads to liberation. First he visited the Indian town of Sarnath, where he taught the quintessence of Buddhism: the Four Noble Truths. This sermon marks the beginning of a long period of preaching, known by Buddhists as the 'setting in motion of the Wheel of Truth'. Upon hearing the words of the sermon, his companions – former ascetics – became the first Buddhist monks.

More and more people came to hear the Buddha's teachings, because he welcomed anyone who wished to listen, regardless of caste. To the Buddha, 'no one is pariah by birth, no one is Brahmin by birth'; only actions determine the condition of beings. The four decades that followed, punctuated with journeys, rests and retreats, remain historically vague and lack an accurate chronology. The Master's speeches, maxims and reflections (authentic or apocryphal) constitute the only records from this era.

Sensing that his task was complete and that his ultimate departure was near, the Buddha declared to his entourage, 'transient are all conditioned things. Try to accomplish your aim with diligence. Within three months' time, the Perfected One will enter Nirvana. The end of my life is near. ... Live forever in saintliness; resolutely ... . He who lives steadfastly loyal to the words of the Truth ... shall be freed of suffering'. Tradition has it that Gautama died at the age of 80 in Kusinagara. His last words, before reaching the ineffable peace of Nirvana, recall an important element of the Buddhist doctrine: 'Perhaps, my friends, you are thinking: "We no longer have a Master?" But you mustn't think this. The Law remains the Law as I taught you; may it guide you when I am no longer with you. ... Work out your own salvation, with diligence.'

THE BUDDHIST DOCTRINE AND ITS MEANING

Initially transmitted orally after the Buddha's death, his words (probably spoken in Magadhi, a Middle Indian dialect), were recorded in the Pali language, by Buddhist monks in Ceylon (present-day Sri Lanka) in the canonical texts (Tipitaka or 'Three Baskets'). Written over four centuries after the Master's demise (the acknowledged date is 89 BC), these sacred books contain the Buddha's speeches or texts of the Law (sutra), monastic regulations (vinaya) and scholastic treatises.

At the dawn of the third millennium, we should consider what the Buddhist doctrine represents. Firstly, inner feelings play a vital role in the Buddhist experience. The teachings of the current Dalai Lama remind us that 'in human society, kindness, love for one's fellow man and compassion are what are most important. They are truly precious and necessary in life.' Unlike the great monotheist traditions (Judaism, Christianity and Islam), Buddhism does not refer to a divine revelation. Individual experience is central to its practice. This 'inner science' or rule of life teaches that all mortals are equal in suffering. In the face of human anguish, the Buddha, Siddharta Gautama, exemplified how, by renouncing desires and eliminating ignorance, one could obliterate this ocean of suffering.

To free oneself from the hustle and bustle of life, the Buddhist approach stresses inner contemplation, wisdom and compassion, and separates the duality of body and soul. Buddhism does not offer an ethical theory divorced from action: compassion, loving kindness and wisdom have to be cultivated and enacted in daily life. The Buddha emphasises that the path he describes is a path of mental transformation. Knowledge is only seen to be useful if it is tied to this path of transformation. The path that the Buddha teaches is a way of turning unwholesome actions based on greed, hatred and delusion into wholesome acts based on generosity, compassion and wisdom. This is why the quality of the intention behind any action

is considered to be of paramount importance. In addition, an incorrect relationship with the self and with others is a positive hindrance to development on the Buddhist path. This means that if one holds to the egocentric notion of a permanent and abiding self then one can never come into a genuinely open relationship with others, because there will always be the tendency to place one's own needs and desires before those of others. According to this view, authentic compassion for others would be almost impossible to bring into being.

The first teaching of the Buddha concerned each person's predisposition to suffering. Through the Four Noble Truths, he examined the nature of suffering, its cause, its end and the path to its cessation.

THE FOUR NOBLE TRUTHS

The First Noble Truth is the Noble Truth of Suffering. Birth, sickness, old age and death are suffering. Pain, grief, sorrow, lamentation and despair are suffering. Association with what is unpleasant, disassociation from what is pleasant and not realising one's desires are suffering. In short, clinging to the five aggregates leads to suffering. Human existence is a composite of the five aggregates (*khandhas*): corporeality or physical form, feelings or sensations, perception, mental formation (conditioned responses to one's experiences and the idea of self) and consciousness.

The First Noble Truth is a diagnosis of the human condition, a statement of our sickness. In Buddhist tradition, the Buddha is often likened to a spiritual physician who offers us a diagnosis and then a cure. As such, the First Noble Truth encourages individuals to examine their own position with regard to the dissatisfaction and suffering they encounter in their daily lives.

THE MASTER AND HIS DISCIPLES
This scene from the Buddha's life, painted in China during the tenth century, depicts the Buddha teaching his disciples.

The First Noble Truth teaches that all forms of existence are inevitably subject to suffering. This means that in the cycle of life, joy does not endure and the sadness that stems from the prospect of suffering obscures moments of well-being. The transitory aspect of a life punctuated with joys that invariably end, torments the human mind. The instability and imperfection of things are intolerable. This statement, sometimes judged in the West to be extremely pessimistic or even fatally hopeless, in fact encourages individuals to cultivate their 'Buddhist nature', and to follow Gautama's example.

The Second Noble Truth states that there is a cause of suffering. From the Buddhist perspective, this is where we can begin to move from diagnosis to the possibility of a cure: if there is a cause, then it can be identified and eliminated, and the effect, suffering, will cease. The Buddha identifies the cause of suffering to lie in craving or 'thirst', fuelled by an underlying delusion about the fundamental nature of reality.

The Third Noble Truth shows that there is an end to suffering. 'It is the utter cessation of this thirst [arising out of selfish desires], the withdrawal from it, the renouncing of it, the rejection of it, non-attachment to it.' Ridding oneself of wrong perceptions, eliminating mental cravings and unwholesome thoughts is of supreme importance in Buddhism. The elimination of desire is the complete opposite of its repression, as understood in the psychoanalytic traditions, and removing sources of obstruction has become the aim of the practising Buddhist. Western behaviour – as observed in some aspects of the Judaeo-Christian ethic and psychoanalytical research – on the other hand, often tends to confuse the elimination of desire with repressing it or holding it back. The effect of this, in the Buddhist tradition, is a new source of suffering, which amounts to psychosis or neurosis. One must then examine whether, in Buddhist terms, there is a way to escape this oppressive inclination.

The Fourth Noble Truth can be seen as a rule of life for practising Buddhists. It avoids the two extremes of indulging desires and self-mortification. It shows us the path, the 'Middle Way', which leads to cessation of suffering. This is known as the Noble Eightfold Path – an entirely practical path – divided into three aspects: wisdom, morality and meditation. Right View and Right Intention constitute the path of wisdom, while Right Speech, Right Action and Right Livelihood comprise the path of morality. Finally, there is the path of meditation, which consists of Right Mindfulness and Right Concentration. This is a practical path, because it is not founded on metaphysical principles. It indicates that there is a basic relationship between one's understanding, actions and underlying emotional state. As a general rule, the Buddha criticised the propensity to engage in metaphysical or philosophical speculation as not conducive to the task with which he was concerned – the elimination of suffering and unsatisfactoriness. He taught that to transform the world of suffering one must transform one's own nature. This could be achieved through the practice of morality and meditation, by following five basic moral precepts: to refrain from harming living things, to refrain from taking what is not given, to refrain from false speech, to refrain from sexual misconduct and to refrain from taking substances which cloud the mind and which cause one to break the other four precepts.

GRECO-BUDDHIST ART

The figure's posture and drapery reveal the Greek origins of this bodhisattva representation.

KARMA, *SAMSARA* AND NIRVANA: PILLARS OF THE BUDDHIST DOCTRINE

Buddhist practice begins with 'seeking refuge' in the Three Jewels: the Buddha, the dharma (the law) and the *sangha* (the community). According to the current Dalai Lama: 'the Buddha is the Master who shows us the path to Enlightenment, the *dharma* is the true refuge where we seek protection from suffering, and the *sangha* is made up of spiritual companions who follow the stages of the path.'

THE DEATH OF THE BUDDHA

According to tradition, the Buddha lay down just before his death. Deep in sorrow, his disciples were unaware of the state of supreme deliverance their master had reached, a state of being that is referred to as Parinirvana and which marks the end of the cycle of rebirth.

The Noble Eightfold Path depends on karma, which guides the unenlightened being through the eternal cycle of death and rebirth (*samsara*). In a similar way to the pre-Buddhist Brahmin and Vedic beliefs, karma (law of action) describes a cause-and-effect relationship: every action has an effect. Actions are of three kinds: actions of the body, actions of speech and actions of the mind. Whenever we commit an action in thought, word or deed we set up a chain reaction of causes and effects that have no predictable outcome. An action that we commit now might not come to fruition within this lifetime, but will actually ripen in another lifetime. The only thing that we can say with any certainty is that all actions have consequences. The law of cause and effect often creates misunderstanding in contemporary Western thought by confusing the factor that triggers an action and the true underlying cause of that action. For example, if someone addresses you in a disagreeable manner, they are not the ultimate cause of your anger. Their behaviour reveals a facet of your character. It is your own responsibility to search for the source of your reaction, in order to behave differently in similar unpleasant situations. Understanding the cause of your actions can change the karmic pattern of your life.

The *samsara*, or cycle of rebirth, is influenced by karma. Inherently unsatisfying, because there is no prospect of progressing to a happier afterlife, it is characterised by emptiness, illusion and suffering. The circle of *samsara* leads the consciousness to transmigrate from one existence to another. The principle of *samsara*, like karma, is found in other Indian traditions that predate Buddhism, where again it features as a perpetual carrier of suffering.

In the Buddhist tradition, Nirvana can be seen as extinguishing the fires of greed, hatred and delusion that keep us bound to the wheel of rebirth. It is a state of peace where no more unwholesome karma can be generated. However, it ought to be stressed that Nirvana is not a place, but a state of mind.

In a more specialised sense, according to Tibetan Buddhist tradition, Nirvana signifies deliverance, complete extinction, the end of the cycle of rebirth, and thus of suffering. It is a state of perfect unity so subtle that it cannot be described adequately in words. To attain Nirvana – the ultimate end of rebirth – one must renounce desire (as manifested in the five aggregates) and detach oneself from both existence and non-existence. According to the great Tibetan Buddhist masters, Nirvana exists as a state of supreme voidness and absolute completion, which is liberation and genuine peace. Those who attain Enlightenment (Awakening) will reach Nirvana.

BUDDHIST TOLERANCE

The community of the first Buddhist disciples and followers was divided into many branches. The impetus to spread the word according to the Buddha's instructions led practitioners to adapt the teachings over time to fit the needs of different cultures. Buddhism has never undergone drastic or radical schisms during its 2,500-year evolution, but the different branches have adapted to the local historical, cultural, political and economical context. The various schools of Buddhism agree to differ on points of doctrine, and relationships between the various groups are generally good. Their disputes have remained at the level of lively discussion and have degenerated into more serious conflicts only when involving questions of economics or politics. Buddhism is also tolerant towards other faiths.

MANDALAS

These are paintings or drawings representing a sacred place. They are a source of inspiration and meditation for Buddhists.

THE THREE MAIN SCHOOLS OF BUDDHISM

The Theravada (Hinayana) school: The term 'Hinayana' is usually frowned on these days, because Mahayana Buddhists have used it as a pejorative term to refer to non-Mahayanist schools. Hinayana literally means 'Lesser Vehicle' (as opposed to the Mahayana 'Greater Vehicle'). It is practised by the majority of Buddhists in Sri Lanka, the Union of Myanmar (formerly Burma), Thailand, Cambodia, Laos and South Vietnam. Many people now prefer the less disparaging terms: 'Theravada', 'School of the Ancients', or Southern School of Buddhism. Of the many non-Mahayanist schools that have existed, Theravada is the only one that has survived up to the present day.

The Mahayana school (Northern School of Buddhism): This is practised mainly in China, Korea, Japan, Tibet and North Vietnam. It was given its name, which means 'Greater Vehicle,' because its followers believed that it was a way of accommodating all types of believers, rather than a few select monks, nuns and priests.

The Mahayanist movement transcends the limitations of personal salvation by associating it with beings of infinite compassion, the bodhisattvas. A bodhisattva (a being devoted to Enlightenment) is spiritually perfect, but dedicates his/herself to the attainment of full and perfect buddhahood for the benefit of all sentient beings. The bodhisattva foregoes the goal of becoming an arhat in order to help sentient beings, thus committing him/herself to endless rebirths in the cycle of death/rebirth (*samsara*) in order to attain this goal. A Mahayanist disciple aspires to become a bodhisattva, devoted to helping others advance towards deliverance, and even to become a buddha. Mahayanists believe that anyone can escape from *samsara* and attain Enlightenment – thus, given the right conditions, anyone can become a buddha.

The Mahayanist quest for Enlightenment involves the practice of six perfections or *paramita*: generosity, morality, patience, diligence, meditation, and transcendental wisdom. Altruism and the quest for happiness for all individuals characterise this approach.

Some of the buddhas arising out of different branches of Buddhism personify energies, covering principles such as wisdom, compassion or the power to heal. Mahayana tradition states that there were a number of other human buddhas who lived before the historical Buddha. Six buddhas are said to have preceded Gautama; they are collectively known as the Tathagata (meaning 'Those who have gone beyond'). Probably the most important is the buddha who existed immediately prior to Siddharta Gautama – Dipankara.

The Vajrayana school: The Vajrayana, or 'Diamond Vehicle', is practised in Tibet, Mongolia and Bhutan, as well as in the Indian and Nepalese regions of the Himalayas. It shares the same outcome as the aforementioned movements, but it incorporates the Hindu religious belief of Tantrism. Buddhist Tantrism apparently originated in northern India, and was passed on orally in the third century AD. The difference in the Vajrayana school lies in the methods used to reach wisdom. The Vajrayanists use meditative and physical practices, particularly yoga exercises and visualisation of deities by means of drawings called mandalas, or they recite sacred formulas known as mantras, with mystical values that reinforce the energetic power of the words. In the Vajrayana, one must receive a ritual and oral initiation (literally an 'empowerment') from a spiritual master. The 'Diamond' of Diamond Vehicle implies unsplittable, meaning either a continuity of vows and pledges, a continuous master–disciple lineage, or the unbroken practice of the doctrine.

Vajrayanists maintain that all experiences are manifest and sacred expressions of the enlightened spirit. Thus, transforming one's weaknesses into strengths, rather than struggling against them, is seen to be a means of spiritual liberation. Knowledge of the tantras and the practice of esoteric rituals all contribute towards the transformation of an individual's body, mind and speech. Thus, Tantric rituals are seen as a harmonisation of these elements directed towards the Buddhist goal of awakening.

TIBET

Lobsang Gyatso (1617–82), the fifth Dalai Lama, political and spiritual unifier, wise diplomat and tolerant monk, was an incarnation of the highest authority in Tibet.

THE BUDDHIST INFLUENCE THROUGHOUT ASIA

According to tradition, the first three Buddhist Councils were held in each of the first three centuries following the death of the Buddha. The first Council is believed to have been held around 477 BC, in a cave in Rajagrha (north-east India), where a code for the Buddhist doctrine was drawn up with the help of Ananda, the Master's cousin and preferred disciple. A split occurred in the monastic sangha during the second Council, held in Vaisali (north-west Bihar) around 377 BC. It was divided into two schools, each with its own traditions of ordination. According to modern scholars, the split was caused by a disagreement over the vinaya (monastic rules). Some of the monks wished to tighten these rules, while the majority was happy to leave things as they were. It resulted in the sangha being divided into the Theravada and the Mahsanghikas (the Great Community).

At the third Council, around 241 BC, believed to have been held in Pataliputra (present-day Patna), a further split occurred on the subject of Abhidharma (the interpretation of Buddhist psychology). The accounts of this dispute are somewhat confused and misleading and it is highly likely that this further split was occasioned by another disagreement over monastic rules.

The doctrine of the Enlightened One spread as far as northern India, Kashmir and Afghanistan, and, over a period of several centuries, even penetrated the kingdoms of Bactria, once part of Alexander the Great's empire. Buddhist dissemination continued until the seventh to eighth centuries AD. The initial spread involved the non-Mahayanist schools, including the Theravada, with the Mahayana school emerging later. Buddhism prospered in Ceylon before reaching the countries of South-East Asia: the kingdom of Siam (present-day Thailand) (see Ayudhya, p. 84), the Khmer kingdom and its principalities (see Angkor, p. 84), Laos, South Vietnam and part of the Indonesian archipelago.

ZEN

Silence lies at the core of Japanese Zen Buddhism. The gardens of the Myoshinji temple in Kyoto are an ideal setting for meditation.

Parallel to this southward movement, advocates of the Greater Vehicle introduced Buddhism into China in the third century, via the Central Asian Silk Road. For the first time in its history, Chinese civilisation was exposed to foreign thought. Despite strong opposition from the followers of Confucianism, conversion to Buddhism reached its peak during the Tang dynasty (618–907 AD). In the fourth century, Buddhism moved on to Korea and later to Japan.

BUDDHISM IS DRIVEN FROM ITS BIRTHPLACE

Over a period of about 1,000 years, Buddhism spread slowly but surely throughout Asia. Although it may have conquered Eastern Asia, it failed to thrive in its country of origin. By the seventh century AD, many of the Buddhist monasteries of northern India had been destroyed by the Huns, the Persian Muslims and, above all, the Brahmins. The various Muslim invasions, over a period of about 300 years, destroyed the large monasteries that had acted as power bases for the Buddhist communities. Even so, Buddhism did not completely disappear from northern India until the 13th century AD, and, in southern India, which was relatively unaffected by the Muslim incursions, it clung on until the 18th century.

TIBETAN BUDDHISM

According to Tibetan tradition, in the seventh century AD, the Tibetan king, Songtsen Gampo, took two wives – a Nepalese and a Chinese princess – both of whom were practising Buddhists.

The marriage was probably a rather shrewd political move rather than motivated by any religious concerns—a calculated attempt to appease the powerful Chinese dynasty. Each princess brought with her a priceless image of Buddha, dating from the time of Siddharta Gautama. They had two temples built to house the images, and these became the focus and foundation for the great Buddhist tradition in Tibet.

The integration of Buddhism into Tibetan culture took place over at least three centuries. The Tibetan Buddhists took over elements of the indigenous Bon religion, and utilised many of its symbols and deities, although giving them a Buddhist flavour. Despite some initial resistance all three Buddhist movements (Theravada, Mahayana and Vajrayana) became integrated into one. Tibetan Buddhism is now made up of four main schools and their numerous subdivisions. The four schools were formed at different times, each incorporating elements of the magical tradition of Bon.

BUDDHISM IN JAPAN

The Japanese discovered Gautama's teachings during political, cultural and commercial exchanges with their neighbours almost 1,000 years after the doctrine began. Buddhism arrived via China and Korea around the sixth century AD. The Greater Vehicle was widely adopted, introducing a practical and moral philosophy that brought with it a coherent vision of humankind in the universe. Strictly speaking, there is no Japanese Buddhism, but rather a multitude of movements, schools, sects and subsects that adhere to different interpretations of the Buddhist texts. Shinto, the original, shamanistic Japanese religion is yet another addition to the many 'paths of the Buddha'. Shintoists revere *kami* (divine spirits) and the forces of nature. The deities, who, according to tradition, number amongst the millions, are believed to live in all the plant and mineral elements of Japan.

THE EMERGENCE OF ZEN

Alongside Amidism, and the Nichiren sect, which bases its doctrine on the Lotus Sutra (the major text of the Mahayana), emerged another path to knowledge, Zen. Familiar in the West, this term has caused much ink to flow over the years, and continues to be the subject of both confusion and misinterpretation. Zen is first and foremost a school of meditation – a technique to access directly the state of Buddhist Awakening (Enlightenment). Zen originated in India, where it is called dhyana, and along with the Buddha's teachings, was first introduced to China around 520 AD (during the Middle Empire) by the Indian monk Bodhidharma, where it became known as Ch'an. After moving into Korea, Zen underwent various transformations before firmly establishing itself. Its arrival in Japan dates back to the 12th century.

Silence is central to the Japanese Zen tradition, which advocates self-realisation above all else. If its followers seek perfection, they will be able to find it on their own in daily life. This intuitive and direct experience of the truth cannot be grasped in thought or writing. Okakura Kakuzo, the famous author of *The Book of Tea*, believes that the special contribution of Zen to Eastern thought is its recognition of the mundane as being of equal importance to the spiritual . There is no distinction between great and small. An atom contains as many possibilities as the universe.

In ninth-century China, government suppression of Buddhist monasticism led to the disbanding of all but two schools – the Lin Chi ('Rinzai' in Japanese) sect and the Ts'ao Tung ('Soto' in Japanese) sect. During the 12th century, after visiting China, the monk Eisai brought Rinzai to Japan. This form of Zen perpetuates an exercise known as a koan (an enigma given to the disciple by the master) in order to attain satori (enlightenment). Koans can be seen as parables – folk stories, anecdotes and narratives enriched with insightful comments and poems, which challenge the disciple's intellect while acting as blueprints for various mental exercises and aiding meditation.

After four years' travelling in China to learn about Ch'an teachings, Master Dogen, a Buddhist monk, renowned thinker and disciple of Eisai, established the Soto sect of Zen, in the eighth century. This school promotes silent meditation in the seated position (zazen). The two schools of Zen have had strong aesthetic influences on Japanese painting, ceramics, literature, architecture and gardens. Erich Fromm summarises Zen Buddhism as a combination of the abstraction and rationality of India and the realism and practicality of China.

BUDDHISM IS TAKING THE WEST BY STORM

The 20th century was the century of Auschwitz and Hiroshima, of terror and of hope, of utopias and of materialism – as much Marxist as capitalist – plunging humanity into the unspeakable. In spite of, or perhaps because of, the pre-millennial angst and the global information revolution, Buddhism has been taking the West by storm.

A surrogate for orphans of failed ideologies, escapism for those let down by the Church, or a fashionable belief for New Age followers – whatever the reason, the authentic spiritual search of Buddhism is attracting more and more men and women. In Europe and in the United States, mainly Japanese and Tibetan masters are opening centres and teaching their schools' precepts to an ever-expanding audience. Meanwhile, opportunists are seizing the chance to market the craze for Buddhism. Its appeal to Westerners may lie in its emphasis on experience rather than belief. Siddharta Gautama taught about the path to liberation from suffering without asking his followers to believe in a God or, for that matter, to believe in him. He simply called upon those who were interested to test the validity of his teaching. In a culture that is often spiritually destitute and radically secular, this is an immensely appealing message.

LOOK

THE JAPANESE CITY OF NARA WAS HOME TO THE IMPERIAL COURT UNTIL 794, WHEN THE IMPERIAL FAMILY MOVED TO KYOTO. IN NARA, THE MOST INFLUENTIAL BUDDHIST SCHOOLS PRODUCED – SOME OF THE MOST REMARKABLE WORKS OF BUDDHIST ART IN JAPAN.

Jizo-Bosatsu: bronze polychrome, 12th century, DenKoji temple, Nara.

Shaka-Nyorai: *wood and gold leaf, 13th century, Saidaiji temple, Nara.*

Miroku-Bosatsu*: close-up of hand, tenth century, Koryuji temple, Kyoto.*

Miroku-Bosatsu*: close-up of statue, early seventh century, Koryuji temple, Kyoto.*

Asura, *one of the eight protectors of the Buddha, hollow dry lacquer, eighth century, Kofudaiji temple, Nara.*

Amida-Nyorai (the buddha Amitabha): close-up of an 11th-century gilded bronze, Byodoin temple, Kyoto.

Yakushi-Nyorai: *right side of face, wood, ninth century, Jingoji temple, Kyoto.*

Senyu-kannon: close-up of hands, eighth century, Toshodaiji temple, Nara.

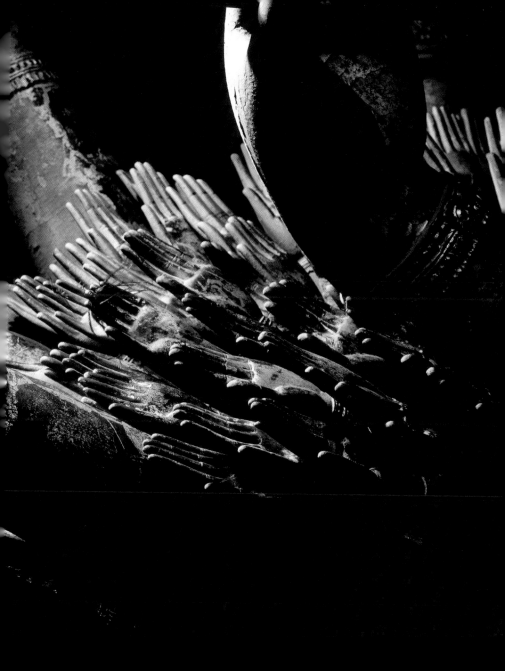

Miroku-Bosatsu (Maitreya): *close-up, wood, seventh century, Chuguji temple, Nara.*

Head of the Yamadadera buddha: *bronze, seventh century, Kofukuji temple, Nara.*

Asura: left side of head, eighth century, Kofukuji temple, Nara.

Ganjin Wajo, *Tang priest, hollow dry lacquer, eighth century, Toshodaiji temple, Nara.*

IN PRACTICE

THE SYMBOLISM OF BUDDHIST ART AND THE GESTURES OF THE BUDDHAS.
STUPAS AND MANDALAS. THE MOST IMPRESSIVE ARCHITECTURAL SITES – FROM
BOROBUDUR TO PAGAN. JAPANESE ZEN GARDENS. BUDDHIST FESTIVALS IN THE
HIMALAYAS. ZEN AND THE ART OF ARCHERY.

In the footsteps of the Buddha

From birth to death, the major stages in the life of Siddharta Gautama graphically illustrate the origins of Buddhism.

SARNATH – WHERE THE BUDDHA GAVE HIS FIRST SERMON

The Buddha preached the basis of the doctrine – the Four Noble Truths – to his followers near Benares in north-east India, in a deer park located in the inner suburbs of Sarnath. Historically, this sermon forms the core of Buddhist thought, and a great raised stupa was built to mark the site. There was a pond to the east of the park where, according to ancient accounts, Gautama liked to bathe.

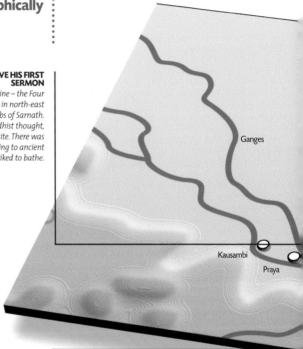

Ganges

Kausambi

Praya

BODH GAYA – PLACE OF ENLIGHTENMENT

On the banks of the river Nirandjana, in the state of Bihar in north-east India, there lies a small village called Bodh Gaya. This is where Siddharta Gautama became the Buddha by gaining enlightenment. At the time, he was seated beneath a pipal tree, which has since become known as the Bodhi tree (which means 'awakening to knowledge'). The first Buddhist monastery was founded here and around the seventh century AD, the Mahabodhi temple was first erected as a monument for pilgrims to celebrate this most sacred of places.

LUMBINI – WHERE THE BUDDHA WAS BORN

On 4 February 1996, the Nepalese Prime Minister Sher Sahadur Deuba officially designated Lumbini as the birthplace of the historical Buddha. The discovery of a stone from a brick chamber in the ruins of the Maya monastery confirms earlier speculation that this was the correct site (it was first noted in 249 BC by the Emperor Asoka).
The famous Japanese architect Kenzo Tange – renowned for his work on the Olympic stadium in Tokyo (1964), the Hiroshima Peace Park and Centre (1956) and, more recently, the new Tokyo City Hall Complex (1991) – has been commissioned to build the Centre for International Buddhist Culture and Learning in Lumbini.

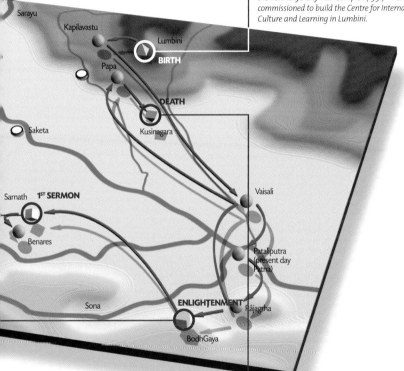

The four sites of importance in the life of the Buddha.

KUSINAGARA – WHERE THE BUDDHA PASSED AWAY

Although a tireless traveller, the Buddha died in the land of his childhood. He spent his final days in the town of Kusinagara in eastern Uttar Pradesh. After his demise, his remains were cremated and his ashes shared amongst different officials. According to tradition, the Buddha's relics are respectfully preserved in various stupas.

The spread of Buddhism

There were various routes along which Buddhism spread through Asia. The great trade routes, the legendary Silk Roads, ran from India to the Great Wall of China. The Buddhist influence was also conveyed via the southern waterways. Spurred on by the Emperor Asoka, Ceylon (present-day Sri Lanka – 'Buddhism's eldest daughter') became a key area through which the religion was disseminated in the Far East. The monks and scholars responsible for spreading Buddhism were largely self-taught, and overcame numerous pitfalls and obstacles in their quest to pass on Buddhist teachings.

In the West

In the 19th century, Buddhism was first brought to the attention of Westerners mainly through the works of the German philosopher, Arthur Schopenhauer, and later through other European and American scholarly works. However, Buddhist thought remained primarily in the realm of specialists and certain esoteric movements. Then, in the first half of the 20th century, accounts of travel writers started captivating the attention of a generation in search of individual freedom. The arrival of Japanese and then Tibetan masters in the 1950s facilitated more direct contact with the doctrine and with Eastern societies. The charismatic personality of the Dalai Lama and the growing number of Buddhist centres on both sides of the Atlantic reinforced a general interest in Buddhist philosophy. This, in turn, has been strengthened by the search for greater meaning in life, as an antidote to materialism.

BANGLADESH

SRI LANKA

the main lines of Buddhist dissemination

the routes followed by Chinese pilgrims

NEPAL

INDIA

MONGOLIA

The diagrams indicate the percentage (in blue) of Buddhists in the different Asian countries.

60

How many Buddhists are there worldwide?

There are nearly 15 million followers in Europe, two to three million in the US and 350 million worldwide – the figures are difficult to verify. Until the 1960s Buddhism in Britain tended to be confined to thinkers and those who had the time to explore different philosophies. However, with the age of Flower Power came the desire to lead a gentle, non-confrontational lifestyle and, added to the general interest in Eastern cultures, Buddhism began to attract followers from all sections of society. In America, first the Beat and then the Hippie movements inspired the same kind of interest, popularised by literary figures such as Jack Kerouac and Allen Ginsberg. Meanwhile, this activity in the materialistic West began to encourage a revival in the East, where, in India, Buddhism had been in decline.

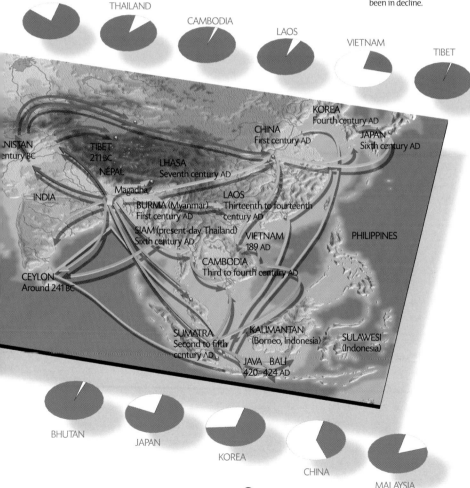

MYANMAR (BURMA)

THAILAND

CAMBODIA

LAOS

VIETNAM

TIBET

KOREA
Fourth century AD

CHINA
First century AD

JAPAN
Sixth century AD

AFGHANISTAN
...century BC

TIBET
211 BC

LHASA
Seventh century AD

NEPAL

Magadha

INDIA

BURMA (Myanmar)
First century AD

LAOS
Thirteenth to fourteenth century AD

SIAM (present-day Thailand)
Sixth century AD

VIETNAM
189 AD

PHILIPPINES

CAMBODIA
Third to fourth century AD

CEYLON
Around 241 BC

SUMATRA
Second to fifth century AD

KALIMANTAN
(Borneo, Indonesia)

SULAWESI
(Indonesia)

JAVA BALI
420–424 AD

BHUTAN

JAPAN

KOREA

CHINA

MALAYSIA

The Silk Roads

The Silk Roads aided the spread of Buddhism throughout Central Asia and China. The cruel desert lands traversed by these routes were dotted with oases, which became important centres of Buddhist culture.

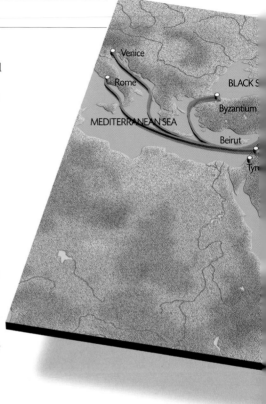

Silk, gold and precious gems

The Buddhist monasteries constructed along the Silk Roads also played their part as fortresses and caravanserais (watering places for caravans). The caves in these regions harbour thousands of Buddhist manuscripts, paintings and statues. Merchants coveted the precious Chinese merchandise – the legendary silk, as well as gold, precious gems, furs and spices. They also co-operated closely with the Buddhist monks. This mixing of monks and laity helped to develop and transmit Buddhist ideas, facilitating the spread of the doctrine across the immense Eurasian trading area.

At the heart of Central Asia

Beginning in the third century AD, Chinese monks in search of the fundamental Buddhist texts journeyed along the famous roads of Serindia, an ancient land that stretched from Iran to China and was bordered at the south by India. Faced with unknown dangers, seventh-century Chinese pilgrims braved perilous journeys across the desert sands, over snow-covered mountain passes and through the lush oases of Central Asia, all to reach India. Later, long after Islam had supplanted Buddhism in the Near East, the archaeological missions of the late 19th and early 20th centuries, particularly those led by Aurel Stein (Britain) from and Paul Pelliot (France), would uncover Buddhist treasures that had lain forgotten for centuries.

The Silk Roads crossed a vast expanse of land – from Persia to the Chinese Empire, and from Mongolia to the Himalayas.

CASPIAN SEA

ARAL SEA

Baghdad
Hamadan
Kasvin
Teheran
Damghan
Mary
Samarkand
Frunze
Yining
Urumqhi
Gobi Desert
Yangi
Turfan
Hami
Kashi
Kuga
Kuga
Louland
Tun-huang
Ejin
Kerman
Kabul
Djalalabad
Shache
Peshawar
Lan-chou
Bandar Abbas
Kandahar
Lahore
Hsien-yang
Mouth of the Indus River
Delhi
OMAN SEA
Ganges Delta

Hiuan-tsang or Xuanzang (602-64)

Xuanzang was probably the most renowned Chinese Buddhist pilgrim. He travelled to all the sacred Buddhist sites in India, his fame spreading far along the Silk Road. His journey across Central Asia took him through Kuchha, Tashkent, Samarkand and Bactria in search of the wellspring of Buddhism. He braved countless dangers to collect many sacred Buddhist scriptures. Two works written by his disciples – Huili and Yancong – *Memoir of the Eastern Countries during the Tang Era* and his biography – recount his adventures.

The buddhas of meditation

Within the cosmic pantheon of the Mahayanic and the Vajrayanic traditions, the five transcendent or meditation buddhas derive from the meditation of the Adibuddha. This is the primordial Buddha, self-born and self-existent, who is comparable to a creator god, in the sense that his teachings are eternally true and unchanging.

AMOGASIDDHI
(North) The All-Accomplishing One. Wisdom of action. Colour: green. Gesture: fearlessness. Element: air. Poison: envy. Emblem on throne: garuda (a mythical figure, half man and half bird).

VAIROCANA
(Centre) The Radiating One, He Who is Like the Sun. All-pervading wisdom. Bodhisattva: Samantabhadra. Colour: white. Gesture: preaching. Element: ether. Poison: delusion and ignorance. Emblem on throne: lion or serpent.

AMITHABA
(West) The Boundless Light. Discriminating wisdom. Bodhisattva: Avalokitesvara. Colour: red. Gesture: meditation. Element: fire. Poison: lust and covetousness. Emblem on throne: goose or peacock.

Attributes of the buddhas of meditation

These buddhas are identified with a particular bodhisattva (enlightened being), colour, gesture, cardinal direction, element, emblem and poison.

AKSOBHYA
(East) The Steadfast One.
Mirror-like wisdom.
Bodhisattva: Vajrapani.
Colour: blue.
Gesture: touching the earth. Element: water.
Poison: hatred and anger.
Emblem on throne: elephant.

RATNASAMBHAVA
(South) The Jewel-Born One.
Wisdom of equality.
Bodhisattva: Ratnapani.
Colour: yellow.
Gesture: giving. Element: earth. Poison: pride.
Emblem on throne: lion or horse.

The postures shown in Buddhist statues

SEATED POSITION
Western-style, knees and feet slightly apart, represents the royal posture.

STANDING POSITION
Viewed from the front, in a peaceful attitude accentuating the impression of serenity, this posture represents supreme sovereignty.

LYING POSITION
This evokes the Great Extinction, the Buddha in Nirvana.

In addition to the Buddha's features, which are characterised by an expression of inner peace and marks of predestination (elongated earlobes, protruding skull, curly hair ritually wound to the right or pulled back in a chignon), Gautama can be identified by one of the four postures in which he is invariably shown, irrespective of which region the statue comes from. Each posture corresponds to a different mental attitude. Ironically, while he was on Earth the Buddha renounced all forms of hero-worship and idolatry, and yet, over time, his followers could not prevent themselves from glorifying him.

CROSS-LEGGED SEATED POSITION
This symbolises concentration.

Hand gestures seen in the statues

DHARMACHAKRA-MUDRA
Gesture of preaching (turning the wheel of the Teaching)

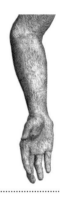

VADARA-MUDRA
Gesture of giving

VITARKA-MUDRA
Gesture of reasoning

ANJALI-MUDRA
Gesture of offering

The literature on hand gestures (*mudra*) is precise in its definitions. In Buddhist iconography, each hand gesture symbolises a different frame of mind. There are over 130 gestures, symbolising such things as respect, welcome, fearlessness and prayer. It is a language borrowed in part from Indian mythology.

ABHAYA-MUDRA
Gesture of protection

DHYANA-MUDRA
Gesture of meditation

PRAJNALINGANABHINAYA
Gesture of embracing

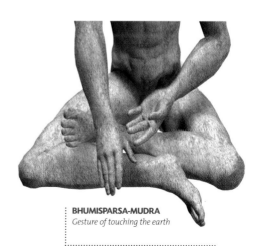

BHUMISPARSA-MUDRA
Gesture of touching the earth

THE TEMPLE, AS SEEN FROM ABOVE

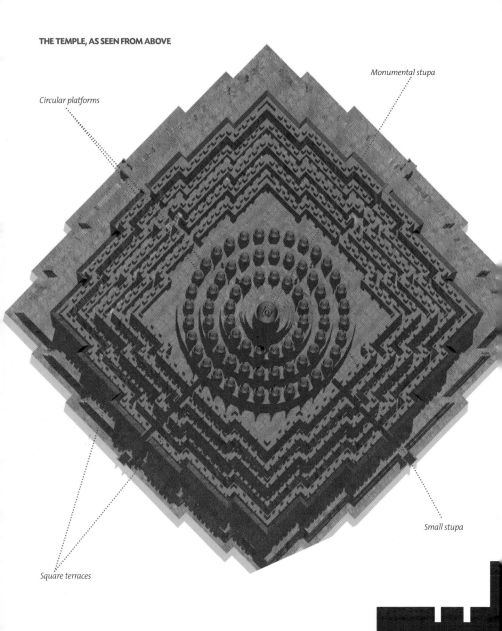

Monumental stupa

Circular platforms

Square terraces

Small stupa

Borobudur – mandala of stone

Built on a hillside, this grandiose pyramidal monument is set in the centre of a volcanic arena, like a jewel of Buddhist art.

Discovery

Borobudur was built between the late eighth and the mid-ninth century in central Java, Indonesia. Its construction was deliberately orientated according to the four cardinal points, and symbolises the earth and sky. After about the 12th century, it lay forgotten, abandoned to the destruction wrought by tropical vegetation and earthquakes, until it was rediscovered by Sir Stamford Raffles in 1894.

A journey of initiation

Borobodur's symbols are many, illustrating the Buddhist law and its wisdom. Although the meaning of some remain obscure, collectively they take us on a journey from the realm of earthly desires and passions via the realm of forms and appearances, finally to reach the world of the divine – a world of formlessness and voidness encompassing a detachment from the physical world. It requires physical as well as spiritual effort to ascend these stages and reach cosmic reality, represented at the summit by a central stupa.

The Borobudur stone mandala comprises three levels: a pyramidal base, including five square terraces, topped by a series of three circular terraces, each smaller than the last, which are then crowned by a monumental stupa. The walls and balustrades of the balconies are decorated with bas-relief illustrations depicting the life of the historical Buddha, to which are added other Indo-Javanese motifs and scenes (*jatakaa*) from the past lives of the Enlightened One.

The circular terraces are lined with seventy-two stupas, each containing a stone statue of the Buddha.

The stupa or chorten

The original stupas (in Sanskrit) or *chortens* (in Tibetan) were dedicated to the Buddha's relics. According to Buddhist tradition, the Buddha was cremated and his ashes were shared amongst eight of his followers. The remains were respectfully preserved in eight stupas, but were later subdivided and distributed to numerous stupas throughout Asia. Later, the ashes of great Buddhist masters would also be buried beneath the stupas.

A place of worship

Stupas are now places of pilgrimage for devout Buddhists, and come in all shapes and sizes, depending on the country and cultural region.

The stupa is a symbol of what is most venerated in the Buddhist world, and may contain sacred scriptures, ritual objects or the ashes of great Buddhist scholars. A pilgrim should pay reverence to a stupa by walking around it several times, keeping it on his or her right hand. In Tibet and the Himalayan kingdoms, a stupa is sometimes raised at the entrance to a village or on the side of a road, to ward off negative forces or evil spirits.

The lower steps of the stupa represent the monastic community (*sangha*).

The square base evokes the teachings passed down from the Enlightened One (the *dharma*).

The sphere resting on top of the structure symbolises the Buddha.

The vertical axis decorated with thirteen discs piled on top of one another symbolises the thirteen suprahuman states, while the stupa as a whole represents the universe.

A chorten in Central Tibet

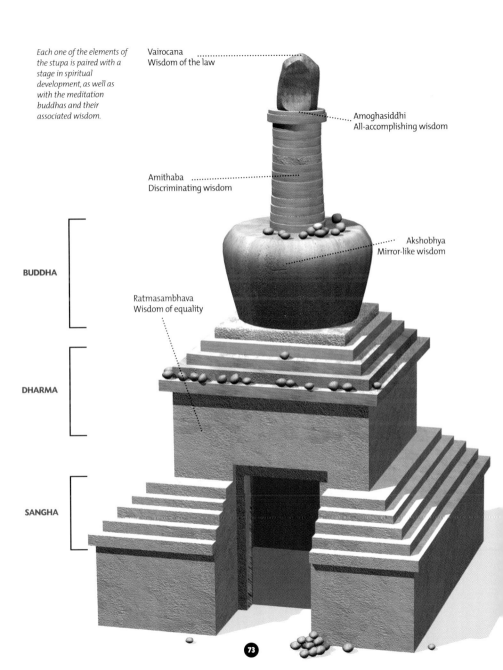

Each one of the elements of the stupa is paired with a stage in spiritual development, as well as with the meditation buddhas and their associated wisdom.

Vairocana
Wisdom of the law

Amoghasiddhi
All-accomplishing wisdom

Amithaba
Discriminating wisdom

Akshobhya
Mirror-like wisdom

Ratmasambhava
Wisdom of equality

BUDDHA

DHARMA

SANGHA

THE MANDALA IS A SACRED DIAGRAM, WITH EACH PART RELATING TO THE UNIVERSE.

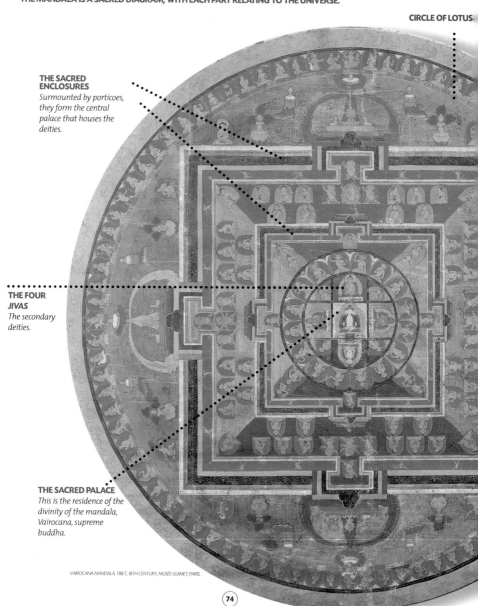

CIRCLE OF LOTUS

THE SACRED ENCLOSURES
Surmounted by porticoes, they form the central palace that houses the deities.

THE FOUR JIVAS
The secondary deities.

THE SACRED PALACE
This is the residence of the divinity of the mandala, Vairocana, supreme buddha.

VAIROCANA MANDALA, TIBET, 18TH CENTURY, MUSÉE GUIMET, PARIS.

The mandala

This Sanskrit word literally means 'circle'. The mandala can be made of stone, coloured sand, or can be painted. It is a representation of the ideal world and is used primarily as an instrument of meditation.

The mandala is a sacred diagram that symbolises the microcosm of psychic energy as well as the cosmic universe. Its colours correspond to the conflicting emotions we must all face: white represents ignorance, red symbolises sexual desire, etc. The main meditational deity generally resides at the heart of the mandala, with the central square housing the secondary deities. The whole picture is contained within one or more concentric circles: the circle of cemeteries, again tied to the world of emotions; the circle of fire, that burns ignorance; the circle of the *vajra*, symbol of stability; and the circle of stylised lotuses, that symbolises a pure conscience. According to one Tantric text, the mandala is the essence of reality itself. Under the guiding authority of a master, practitioners use the mandala in meditation to visualise the steps along the Path to Enlightenment. As Dagpo Rinpoche, a famous Tibetan lama now living in France, explains, 'To choose one's mandala, one must feel drawn to it, like to a person, by that I mean drawn to the figure who occupies the centre and who varies from one mandala to another.'

The Kalachakra mandala

The Kalachakra or 'Wheel of Time' is a tantra that holds a unique place in Tibetan Buddhism. It shows the practices that can lead directly to buddhahood in a single life, taking into account the human body and mind as well as astrological, astronomical and mathematical data. The Kalachakra mandala represents a divine palace, the kingdom of Shambhala, a pure, mythical land deep in the Himalayas, where prosperity and happiness reign. In Kalachakra initiation, conferred by the Dalai Lama, the creation of the mandala as an instrument for meditation is one element of the teaching.

Buddhist festivals in the Himalayas

In Bhutan, a Buddhist state located between Tibet, Sikkim and India, a *tshechu* festival commemorates the man who introduced Vajrayana to the Himalayan regions in the eighth century: Padmasambhava, the famous Indian Tantric master, commonly known as Guru Rinpoche ('precious master').

Tshechus, festivals and celebrations

Depending on the area, *tshechus* can last between three and five days in a row, during which time specific religious dances take place. They are performed either by monks, laity, or *gomchens* (religious laity), and the repertoire is the same almost everywhere. Some *Tshechus* conclude with the veneration of an immense *thangka* (painted banner), which represents Guru Rinpoche and his Eight Manifestations. These spectacular dances – sacred celebrations set to the sound of cymbals, tambourines and long trumpets – trace circles and spirals in a complex and esoteric symbolism of the power of the cosmos and of nature. Some participants draw the Tantric figures of a mandala on the ground, while the feet of the masked dancers pound to the rhythm of the joyous music. The dances glorify Buddhism, purify or protect (shamanism is still alive in the Himalayas), or tell local stories. The religious fervour of these celebrations is tempered by comic sketches.

Monk performing a symbolic dance.

ATSARAS, 'DIVINE MADMEN'	
Atsaras (jesters in smiling masks) improvise and make fun of anything from the sacred dances to the noblemen in the crowd. A mix of the spiritual and the	temporal, these ceremonies are an occasion for the entire population to get together and watch the finely choreographed religious symbolism.

In his book, La Civilisation tibétaine
(Tibetan Civilization, L'Asiathèque, 1987),
Rolf A. Stein describes the dances as
'pantomimes accompanied by music.
Although purely ritual in nature, they
are nonetheless artistic creations –
true theatrical and choreographic
masterpieces. The dance steps are
perfectly co-ordinated down to the last
detail, and the troupe is directed by a
monk who acts as the dance master.'

Dance of the black hats.

The Zen garden

In the 14th century, Japanese Zen monks created a new style of garden: the dry garden. Designed for meditation, it is characterised by its remarkable sand and rock landscaping – a composition often inspired by the Chinese pictorial tradition.

THE ZEN GARDEN OF THE RYOAN-JI BUDDHIST TEMPLE

Built in Ukyo-ku, near Kyoto, Japan, this is one of the most famous Zen gardens. Designed in the 15th century, it is attributed to the renowned landscape artist Soami, who was also a master of the tea ceremony and of flower arrangement (*ikebana*). The expanse of small white pebbles is carefully raked every day by gardeners. The design provokes a calming response, reminding some people of waves, while others see floating clouds. The fifteen stones, of varying shapes and sizes, gathered together in five groups, are set in such a way that the viewer can only see fourteen from any given place in the garden. Although the group as a whole recalls the sacred mountains of China, the individual stones represent the Buddha, a legendary whale, a tigress and her young, a turtle (the incarnation of longevity), and a crane (the winged messenger of the gods). The Ryoan-ji dry garden unites the seven qualities of Zen art: asymmetry, austerity, liberty, the beauty of nature, serenity, simplicity and subtlety.

The eight auspicious signs

In Tibetan culture, these signs are often displayed on religious objects, on banners hung around temples or on curtains in people's homes.

LOTUS FLOWER

The lotus flower grows and blossoms in muddy waters, thus symbolising the possibility for all beings to escape the turmoil of samsara and reach the pure state of deliverance. This deliverance (Nirvana) can only be attained after having purified the body, mind and speech of all imperfections. The lotus flower is also a symbol of tenderness and compassion.

PAIR OF GOLDEN FISHES

The fish is synonymous with liberty and movement. Once an individual has overcome self-dependency, he or she enters a state naturally free of all fear and suffering. Just as the fish swims freely, a fulfilled individual can also live outside of the continual cycle of death and rebirth, thus experiencing the well-being of deliverance.

BANNER OF VICTORY

This symbolises the victory of good and noble actions over obstacles, evil, and negative forces. As part of the dharma, this victory can only be based on self-control found through the quest for sources of suffering within us, and through an individual's inner fulfilment. The banner is also the symbolic representation of ultimate fulfilment.

VASE

The treasure vase represents boundless longevity, prosperity and well-being for all. Boundless well-being is the expression of the state of deliverance from suffering and from the continual cycle of rebirth. At the prosaic level, the vase is a symbol of material wealth and the acquisition of knowledge and good qualities.

CONCH SHELL

The conch shell symbolises the deep, pleasant sound of the teaching of the dharma. The sound of the dharma has the ability to awaken beings from the sleeping state of their ignorance and encourage them to pursue good for themselves and others. At the prosaic level, the conch shell indicates personal influence or an individual's fame.

KNOT

The knot symbolises the union or interdependence of everything. This union is manifest at all levels of reality: in the union of spiritual teaching and secular life and in the way in which Buddhist wisdom and compassion can never be separated; the interdependence of the elements, the indissoluble nature of emptiness and shape; and the union of appearance and unreality. At the prosaic level, the knot symbolises the ties between friendship and brotherhood.

PARASOL

The parasol protects the head from the sun, and is thus synonymous with protection from harm caused by illness, obstacles and negative forces, as well as from any form of suffering endured in the cycle of rebirth (samsara).

WHEEL

The eight-spoked wheel represents the setting in motion of the cycle of the Buddha's teaching. According to Indian tradition, the 'wheel' signifies the Universal King, victorious over all adversaries. It is capable of defeating the sources of confusion and suffering in the world.

A traveller's impressions of Buddhist countries

Temples and pagodas, stupas and monasteries – these wonderful world heritage sites inspire the pilgrims and travellers who come to contemplate them. These sacred monuments, imbued with meaning and serenity, are scattered throughout Asia and exist in a thousand and one forms. Mysterious and sometimes disturbing to Westerners, they have inspired a great many writers and travellers.

 AJANTA

INDIA – THE CAVES OF AJANTA

'The Buddhist statues of Ajanta still convey, in their powerful and weighty serenity, some of the spirituality of feeling that characterises the best of Gupta sculpture. ... There are many figures which admirably transmute into artistic form the mood of Buddhist thought ... They reflect an inward and ambiguous grief which, when one compares it with the agonies of Christian *pietas*, gives an eloquent expression of the essential differences of outlook that part the two great redemptive religions, Christianity and Mahayanist Buddhism.' George Woodcock, *Faces of India*, Faber and Faber, 1964.

BURMA (MYANMAR) – PAGAN

'The number of temples at Pagan almost staggers the imagination. Thousands of temples constructed from brick dot the vast Burmese plain.'

Milton Osborne, *Southeast Asia*, Allen & Unwin, 1997. (The author is a professor, writer, and consultant on Asian issues.)

PAGAN

BURMA (MYANMAR) – SHWEDAGON PAGODA, RANGOON

'The entire pagoda is covered with a coat of gleaming pure gold over half an inch thick, countless squares of fine gold leaf having been donated by the pilgrims who journey there from all over the Buddhist world. Pilgrims believe the Shwedagon is built on the site where eight hairs from the head of Buddha himself are buried.'

Lionel Landry, *The Land and People of Burma*, J. B. Lippincott, 1968. (The author was attaché for *Time* magazine at the American Embassy in Burma and was also the Executive Director of the Asia Society in New York City.)

THAILAND – AYUDHAYA
'Ayudhya was a modest settlement of teakwood houses, surrounded by a mud rampart topped with wooden spikes. But the kingdom was destined to see more than four centuries of imperial splendour, of pageantry and royal pomp, heroism and undying loyalty ...'
Valentin Chu, *Thailand Today*, Thomas Y. Crowell, 1968.

CAMBODIA – ANGKOR THOM, THE BAYON
'I looked up at the tree-covered towers which dwarfed me, when suddenly my blood curdled as I saw an enormous smile looking down on me, and then another smile on another wall, then three, then five, then ten, appearing in every direction.'
Pierre Loti (from La Destination funéraire des grands Monuments khmèrs, *Bulletin de l'École Française d'Extrême-Orient*, 1940), quoted by George Coedès, *Angkor*, Oxford University Press, 1963.

JAPAN – TREASURES OF NARA

'Into this ground – however 'illusory' – of Nara, the doctrine of renunciation plunges its strong and hungry roots. What is left of the temples of this epoch suggests not so much detachment as triumphal affirmation.'
Nicolas Bouvier, *The Japanese Chronicles.*
Mercury House, 1992.

NARA

INDONESIA – BOROBUDUR

'The huge temple of Borobudhur is built on to a slight rounded eminence ... The hill actually forms the core of the temple, which has no interior. It rises by easy stages in conformation to the shape of the knoll. First come two square lower terraces; then four galleries of a rectangular general form, but having twenty angles to allow for the curve of the hill; and finally, four more terraces, the first twelve-angled, the remaining three the outline of the temple ... presents a perfect curve only broken by the projection of its ornamentation.'
Hubert S. Banner, *Romantic Java,* Seeley, Service & Co., 1927.

AYUDHAYA

ANGKOR THOM

BOROBUDUR

Zen and the art of archery

Kyudo ('the way of archery') is an exercise in Zen concentration and requires a high degree of mental discipline. The aim is to strike a perfect balance between body and mind. Before shooting, the archer gathers his or her thoughts; poise and self-possession are indispensable. Good posture and controlled breathing play an important part in this exercise, which some consider to be an art form. Ceremonial gestures also play a part in the noble spiritual training of Zen archery, as codified in texts that date back to the 18th century. The quest for voidness of thought, close to meditation, is applied in fusing one's movements into a fluid whole. The act and the result are one; thus there is no ultimate goal. Hitting the target is not the end of the exercise.

'One must always aim beyond the target. Our whole life, our whole spirit travels with the arrow.'
Master Anzawa

FIND OUT

WHAT IS BUDDHISM? THE LEGEND OF THE BIRTH OF THE BUDDHA.
WHERE TO SEE EXAMPLES OF BUDDHIST ART. A BUDDHIST FABLE.
2,500 YEARS OF BUDDHIST HISTORY. TENZIN GYATSO, THE 14TH DALAI
LAMA AND OTHER PROMINENT FIGURES. MUSEUMS CONTAINING
BUDDHIST ARTEFACTS. ZEN AND THE KOAN. BOOKS, WEBSITES AND
ADDRESSES TO HELP YOU FIND OUT MORE.

What is Buddhism?
Jorge Luis Borges

The clear and scholarly writings of the Argentinian, Borges (1899–1986), constitute one of the best introductions to Buddhist thought. The following excerpt expounds the parable of the man wounded by an arrow.

'Buddhism is, above all, what could be called a *yoga*. What is a *yoga*? It is like the Latin word *jugum* – a yoke, a discipline that people impose on themselves. Among the stories of the Buddha, there is one that is particularly illuminating: the parable of the arrow. A man has been wounded in battle, but he does not want them to remove the arrow. First he wants to know the name of the archer, to what caste he belongs, what the arrow is made of, where the archer was standing at the time, how long the arrow is. While he is discussing these things, he dies. "I, however," said the Buddha, "teach that one must pull the arrow out." What is the arrow? It is the universe. The arrow is the notion of I, of everything to which we are chained. The Buddha is saying that we should not waste time on useless questions. Is the universe finite or infinite? Does the Buddha live after Nirvana or not? All this is useless. What matters is that we pull the arrow out. It is an exorcism, a law of salvation.'

Jorge Luis Borges, translated by Eliot Weinberger, from *Seven Nights*, ©1985 by Eliot Weinberger Reprinted by permission of New Directions Publishing Corp.

The travels of Marco Polo

In Marco Polo's manuscript of 1298, in which he recounted his amazing Asian odyssey, he related the tale of the first Buddha. Although the account seems rather fanciful, it does contain an element of truth.

'This Sakyamuni was the first man in whose name idols were made. According to their traditions he was the best man who ever lived among them, and the first whom they revered as a saint and in whose name they made idols. He was the son of a rich and powerful king. He was a man of such virtuous life that he would pay no heed to earthly things and did not wish to be king. When his father saw that he had no wish to be king or to care for any of the things of this world, he was deeply grieved. He made him a very generous offer: he promised to crown him king of the realm, so that he should rule it at his own pleasure – for he himself was willing to resign the crown and all his authority, so that his son should be sole ruler. His son replied that he would have none of it. When his father saw that he would not accept the kingship for anything in the world, his grief was so bitter that he came near to dying. And no wonder, because he had no other son and no one else to whom he might leave his kingdom. Then the king had recourse to the following scheme. For he resolved to find means of inducing his son to give his mind willingly to earthly things and accept the crown and the kingdom. So he housed him in a very luxurious palace and provided 30,000 maidens of the utmost beauty and charm to minister to him. For no male was admitted, but only these maidens; maidens waited on him at bed and board and kept him company all day long. They sang and danced before him and did all they could to delight him as the king had bidden them. But I assure you that all these maidens could not tempt the king's son to any wantonness, but he lived more strictly and more chastely than before. So he continued to lead a life of great virtue according to their usage.'

The Travels, Marco Polo, translated with an introduction by Ronald Latham, Penguin Classics, 1958.

Words of wisdom

Buddhism is as much a practice as it is a doctrine. To grasp its essence in a few words, through an aphorism or an image, is a perilous exercise – one in which a few followers and religious commentators have indulged nonetheless. Here are some excerpts.

The seeker for perfection must discover in his own life the reflection of the inner light.

Okakura Kakuzo, *The Book of Tea*.

The Buddha does not deliver men, rather, he teaches them to deliver themselves as the Buddha did. They accept his predication of the truth, not because it comes from him, but because his words awaken a personal knowledge that is brought to the light of the mind.

Hermann Oldenberg, *Le Bouddha*.(The Buddha).

If a hundred people sleep and dream, each one of them will experience a different world in his dream. Everyone's dream might be said to be true, but it would be meaningless to ascertain that only one person's dream was the true world and all others were fallacies. There is truth for each perceiver according to the karmic patterns conditioning his perceptions.

Kalu Rinpoche.

When the mind is still, the floor where I sit is endless space.

Muso Soseki.

Buddhism is the science of happiness. It qualifies itself as the extinction of dissatisfaction, of anxiety, of anguish, of pain, of unwellness.

Serge-Christophe Kolm, *Le Bonheur-liberté, Bouddhisme profond et modernité* (Happiness-Freedom, Deep Buddhism and Modernity)..

When you try to understand everything, you will not understand anything. The best way is to understand yourself, and then you will understand everything.

Shunryu Suzuki.

Our understanding of Buddhism is not just an intellectual understanding. True understanding is actual practice itself.

Shunryu Suzuki, Zen Mind, Beginner's Mind..

If we follow the etymology of the word religion, 'what is tied to deity', Buddhism is not a religion, since it does not put forth the idea of a creator god. Is it a philosophy? If, by that, we mean a purely intellectual search for knowledge, then no, it is not a philosophy. But if by this word we mean a certain humanist view of life, a tradition that provides methods for better thought and action then yes, Buddhism is certainly a philosophy.

Dagpo Rimpoche.

Reading words while failing to comprehend practice is like taking medicine but failing to mix the compounds.

Dogen Kigen.

Knowing how to maintain our mind in its own nature, as it is, without being distracted either by outer phenomena or inner thoughts is precisely what we mean by meditation.

Bokar Rinpoche, Meditation, ClearPoint Press, 1993.

The purpose of a fish trap is to catch a fish, and when the fish is caught, the trap is forgotten. The purpose of a rabbit snare is to catch rabbits. When the rabbits are caught, the snare is forgotten. The purpose of words is to convey ideas. When the ideas are grasped, the words are forgotten. Where can I find a man who has forgotten words? He is the one I would like to talk to.

Chuang-Tzu.

My teachings are like a finger pointing at the moon. Do not mistake the finger for the moon.

The Buddha.

Ancient Buddhist legends

Many ancient texts relate the life and teachings of the Buddha. One of the favourite forms of teaching was the parable, as seen in the Khmer story of the tiger and the parrot.

The legend of the birth of the Buddha

According to ancient Indian texts:

Maya had them stop her palanquin in a wood of flowering trees. She got down and walked blithely into the wood. And there she noticed a precious tree, whose branches bent under the weight of its flowers. She drew closer and with her graceful hand pulled down a branch. Suddenly, she was still, and the women who were near her gathered in their arms a beautiful baby. The mother smiled.

At that very moment, all living beings trembled with joy. Singing was heard in the sky, and there was dancing. Trees of all seasons blossomed with flowers and bore ripe fruit. Serenely pure rays of light filled the sky. The sick no longer suffered. The hungry were filled up. Those who had consumed liquor felt sober. The mad regained their reason. The crippled were sound in body. The poor found gold. The prison doors swung open. The mean no longer knew evil.

Tale of the tiger and the parrot (a Khmer story)

In the neighbourhood of the kingdom of Benares lived a tiger with his old father. This tiger was a virtuous creature. He always made sure to provide food for his father. Not far away, lived a parrot who was also very virtuous, who befriended the tiger. One day, a man without virtue wished to travel across the land. At the foot of the mountains, he came across the bird, who greeted him and asked him all sorts of questions. During the conversation, the parrot learned that the man wished to go to Benares and intended to cross the mountains that lay before them. The parrot told him that ferocious tigers lived in the mountains, that he should be cautious and should take another route in order to avoid them. The man was in a hurry and decided to take the shortest route. So the parrot told him: 'If that is so, then take this path. I have a friend who is a tiger. If you encounter him, introduce yourself as one of my friends running an errand for me in Benares.'

The path of the man without virtue

With these words, the man without virtue looked for food before heading on his way. Not satisfied with the fruit that the parrot had given him, by way of thanks he grabbed a stick and killed the parrot, made a fire, roasted the bird and ate it. Then he set off towards the mountain. When the tiger learned that the man was a friend of the parrot, he took him in for the night and left to hunt for food. While the tiger was gone, the man told the father of the tiger how much he had enjoyed the delicious parrot. When the tiger returned with a meal, the man ate to the point of indigestion and then fell asleep. Then, the old father tiger warned his son about the fate of his friend the parrot. In tears, the tiger hurried to where the parrot lived, only to find a few feathers left on the ground. Furious, he decided to devour the man.

The tiger and the parrot are reborn in Nirvana

Not seeing the tiger the next morning, the man without virtue questioned the father tiger and learnt that he had been denounced. So he killed the old animal and waited for the tiger to return so that he could finish him off as well. But, due to the tiger's many virtues, the man could not complete his fatal act. He began to tremble, bowed down before the tiger and begged forgiveness. Seeing his father dead, his head broken in two, the tiger realised what the man had done. Grief-stricken, he immediately thought of rendering justice. But, in addition to his virtuous qualities, the tiger was also intelligent. He looked to the future and knew how to discern beneficial actions from wrongdoings – and was keenly aware of the consequences of the latter. And so he thought, 'This man is without virtue, but is that a reason to make him suffer? The deaths of my friend and my father came about because of the karma they created in their previous lives.' So he answered the murderer in a kindly fashion and accompanied him until he was out of danger. The parrot was reborn in Nirvana, and the tiger, at the end of his life, attained Nirvana as well. Some might find this privilege surprising, since the tiger devoured living beings to feed itself. However, it was the virtue that he demonstrated in such a circumstance that caused his rebirth in Nirvana; and even if this event had not occurred, the tiger would still be in Nirvana, because, according to the Buddhist adage, once death arrives, 'the heart that has acquired merits, the pure heart, is reborn in Nirvana.'

2,500 years of history

The following are key dates in the history of Buddhism, from the birth of Siddharta Gautama in the sixth century BC to the Nobel Peace Prize recently awarded to the Dalai Lama.

Around 563 BC: birth of the Buddha in Lumbini.

Around 483 BC: death of the Buddha in Kusinagara.

Around 477 BC: first Buddhist Council, held in Rajagrha.

Around 377 BC: second Council in Vaisali.

Around 296–232 BC: reign of Asoka, Emperor of India and founder of the Maurya Dynasty. He promoted the spread of Buddhism beyond the borders of his empire by sending missionaries to Ceylon and Burma.

Around 241 BC: third Council in Pataliputra, capital of Magadha.

166–145 BC: governance of the Punjab by the Greek King Menander, protector of Buddhism.

65 AD: introduction of Buddhism to China, via the Silk Road.

First century AD: fourth Buddhist Council.

Around 88: the first Pali scriptures of the Buddhist canon are created in Ceylon.

Around 300: Theravada/Hinayana Buddhism (the School of the Ancients) spreads throughout Thailand.

372: introduction of Mahayana Buddhism to Korea.

Fifth century: introduction of Buddhism to Japan and Laos.

520: the Indian monk Bodhidharma establishes a Buddhist meditation school in China. It becomes known as 'Ch'an'.

527: Mahayana Buddhism becomes the state religion in the kingdom of Silla (Korea).

610: Mahayana Buddhism becomes the state religion in Japan.

618–907: under the Tang Dynasty, Buddhism reaches its zenith in China.

Seventh century: inception of Vajrayana (also known as the 'Diamond Vehicle'). Emergence of Khmer Buddhist art in Cambodia.

Eighth century: Mahayana Buddhism is practised in Indonesia. Borobudur is constructed in Java.

Around 750: Buddhism is instituted in Tibet with the coming of the Indian master Padmasambhava.

Early ninth century: a great number of canonical Buddhist texts are translated into Tibetan.

1181–6: Mahayana Buddhism reaches its peak in Cambodia. Angkor Thom is constructed.

Late 12th century: destruction of Mahayana universities by the Muslims, and opposition from the Brahmin to the doctrine of the Enlightened One.

Late 13th century: in Cambodia, the Mahayana doctrine is supplanted by Theravada in Cambodia, which arrived via the kingdom of Siam.

14th century: first Mongolian conversion to Tibetan Buddhism.

Late 15th century: Indonesia converts from Buddhism to Islam.

1617–82: the fifth Dalai Lama, Ngawang Lobsang Gyatso, orders the construction of the Potala palace, and, as Tibet's first spiritual and temporal leader, unifies the country.

1635–1723: lifespan of Zanabazar, the first great Mongolian spiritual master and famous sculptor.

1871: fifth Buddhist Council in Mandalay, Burma.

1920: revival of Buddhism in Vietnam as a reaction to French colonisation.

1924–37: eradication of Buddhism in Mongolia during the Stalinist Communist Revolution.

1926: founding of the Buddhist Society in England.

1927: Frenchwoman Alexandra David-Neel publishes *My Journey to Lhasa*.

1929: Mlle G. Constant Lounsbery founds the Société des Amis du Bouddhisme (Friends of Buddhism Society) in Paris.

Late 1949: the first soldiers of the Chinese People's Liberation Army invade Tibet, to 'liberate it from the imperialist forces'.

17 May 1954: Sixth Buddhist Council in Rangoon, Burma.

23 May 1956: commemoration of the 2,500th anniversary of the Buddha's birth.

17 March 1959: His Holiness the Dalai Lama flees into exile in India (Dharamsala), together with over 100,000 refugees.

11 June 1963: in Saigon, a monk sets himself on fire, to draw the attention of the world to the violently repressive measures of the President of South Vietnam, Ngo Dinh Diem.

1966–76: the Cultural Revolution in China. Destruction of Tibetan monasteries.

1975: persecution of monks and nuns in Vietnam by the Hanoi government, and in Cambodia by the Khmer Rouge.

1987: violent repression in Lhasa, capital of Tibet, following demonstrations by monks and nuns.

5 October 1989: His Holiness Tenzin Gyatso, the 14th Dalai Lama, is awarded the 1989 Nobel Peace Prize.

1991: a mass grave of Buddhist monks is discovered in Mongolia. They were executed in the 1930s when they were deemed public enemies.

4 February 1996: in Lumbini, the Nepalese Prime Minister Sher Sahadur Deuba officially announces the discovery of a stone indicating the birthplace of the historical Buddha.

5 January 2000: Ugyen Trinley Dorje, the 17th Karmapa, flees Tibet to join the Dalai Lama in Dharamsala.

Dalai Lamas, symbols of compassion

The title Dalai Lama, generally translated as 'ocean of wisdom', was first granted to Sonam Gyatso by the Mongolian Emperor Altan Khan in 1578. His two predecessors were given the title posthumously, so Sonam Gyatso was the third Dalai Lama. As the spiritual authority for Mahayanists and Tibetan Buddhists, the Dalai Lama, also called 'Great Perfection' or Kundun ('Presence'), has become an emblematic figure far beyond the borders of Tibet. The Dalai Lama lineage has continued without interruption since its inception.

The fifth Dalai Lama – diplomat and scholar

Lobsang Gyatso will be remembered by Tibetan history as the 'Great Fifth'. This political and spiritual unifier, a visionary diplomat and eclectic religious figure, was the incarnation of supreme authority in Tibet. He ordered the construction of the Potala palace in Lhasa (the Dalai Lama's residence) and became the first spiritual and secular leader of Tibet in 1642.

The sixth Dalai Lama – poet and libertine

Tsangyang Gyatso is remembered for his transgressions: he left behind the life of a monk for poetry, women and drink.
Below is one of his compositions:

> *The meeting place for me and my love is the dense forest of a southern valley.*
> *Except for the chattering parrot, no one knows about it.*
> *Please, talkative parrot, don't give away our secret.*

Some of his other short poems, translated into English, can be found in *The Turquoise Bee: Love Songs of the Sixth Dalai Lama* (see Bibliography).

The 13th Dalai Lama – realist and visionary

Thoupten Gyatso tried to reform Tibetan society and open up his country at a time when the world was changing faster than the still feudal Tibetan society. The 1904 British colonial expedition led by Colonel Younghusband testifies to the interest of the European powers in a country that was, until then, extremely inward-looking. During this turbulent period in history, the Russians and Chinese also considered the high Himalayan plateaux to be a strategic territory, a buffer between the two great empires of China and India. The 13th Dalai Lama experienced the British Occupation, exile in Mongolia, the damage wrought by the Chinese in Tibet, and finally exile in India, before proclaiming the independence of Tibet in 1913. Despite these hardships and the defiant stubbornness of his entourage, he held fast to his objective to change society. One of his acts, in 1920, was to abolish the death penalty. Just before he died, he announced that a great tragedy would befall Tibet, and was proved right by the Chinese occupation that took place during the time of his successor.

LINEAGE OF THE FOURTEEN DALAI LAMAS

1 Gedun Truppa 1391-1475
2 Gedun Gyatso 1475-1542
3 Sonam Gyatso 1543-1588
4 Yonten Gyatso 1589-1617
5 Ngawang Lobsang Gyatso 1617-1682
6 Tsangyang Gyatso 1683-1706
7 Kelsang Gyatso 1708-1757
8 Jampel Gyatso 1758-1804
9 Lungtok Gyatso 1806-1815
10 Tsultrim Gyatso 1816-1837
11 Khedrup Gyatso 1838-1856
12 Trinley Gyatso 1856-1875
13 Tupden Gyatso 1876-1933
14 Tenzin Gyatso 1935-present

The 13th Dalai Lama, photographed around 1910–12

The 14th Dalai Lama, Tenzin Gyatso

Tenzin Gyatso was only thirteen when Chinese troops invaded Tibet. Since then, he has stood as an unflinching symbol of resistance to oppression.

A life of exile

Born on 6 July 1935 in a small village in the province of Amdo (north-east Tibet), Tenzin Gyatso became the official spiritual leader of the Tibetans when he ascended the 'Lion Throne' in February 1940. Separated from his family at a very young age in order to prepare him for his extraordinary destiny as the guardian of an illustrious Buddhist tradition, he studied under two private tutors. When Chinese Communist troops invaded his country, the inexperienced adolescent found himself confronted with a new Red Mandarin, Chairman Mao. Threats were made to Gyatso's life, and he fled his palace in the Tibetan capital Lhasa on the night of 17 March 1959. Surviving a dangerous 15-day, high-altitude journey, escorted by a handful of followers and freedom fighters, he made his way into India, where Nehru provided a place of sanctuary for him. He settled in Dharamsala, where he has since resided in exile. The day after he was awarded the Nobel Peace Prize in 1989, he gave a lecture and concluded with a short prayer:

For as long as space endures
And for as long as living beings remain
Until then may I too abide
To dispel the misery of the world.

Soul force

As the leader of the Tibetan Buddhists, and spokesman for a nation condemned to oppression by the Beijing authorities, the current Dalai Lama is pursuing an unflagging battle of 'soul force' against the invaders. Inspired by Mahatma Gandhi, he is a steadfast promoter of non-violent action and an ardent environmentalist, who considers himself first and foremost a simple Buddhist monk rather than a great spiritual master.

For His Holiness, dialogue between different spiritual traditions is indispensable. 'The same ideals of love are at the root of all major religions in the world. The Buddha, the Christ, Confucius and Zoroaster all taught love above all. Hinduism, Islam, Jainism, Judaism, the Sikh Law and Taoism share the same goal. The objective of all these spiritual practices is the beneficial development of humanity.' His meetings with the Pope, American rabbis, shamans and religious leaders from the five continents confirm his willingness to unite humanity in religious tolerance.

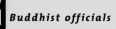

The High Officials of Tibetan Buddhism

At the heart of the teaching of Tibetan Buddhist schools is a tradition that institutionalises the lineage of Buddhist High Officials through reincarnation and lends a relative permanence to the religious order. Now, under the Chinese yoke, the appointment of the Panchen Lama, one such High Official, has entered political and strategic territory.

The Panchen Lama

As a High Official of Tibetan Buddhism, the Panchen Lama ('great scholar') is considered to be an emanation of the buddha Amitabha, and an incarnation of boundless light, invested with spiritual power. The title of Panchen Lama was first given by the fifth Dalai Lama to his religious tutor in 1682.

The current Panchen Lama, prisoner of conscience

Officially recognised on 14 May 1995 by the Dalai Lama as the 11th Panchen Lama, Gedhun Choekyi Nyima, son of a modest Tibetan nomad, born on 25 April 1989, was sent into hiding with his family by the Beijing government in July 1995. This makes him one of the world's youngest prisoners of conscience. His disappearance was orchestrated by the Chinese authorities, officially to protect the child from possible abduction, but in fact aimed at negating the spiritual role of the Dalai Lama. The Chinese, believing that they might influence the choice of a reincarnate lama, then designated another child as the Panchen Lama reincarnated, someone that they wish to manipulate, creating further confusion for the Tibetan people. Many now fear for the life of little Gedhun Choekyi Nyima, whose only fault was to be recognised by the Dalai Lama as a great figure in Tibetan Buddhism.

The Karmapa

Another High Official of Tibetan Buddhism, the Karmapa, head of the Karma-Kagyupa school, holds the power to transmit Enlightenment. The first Karmapa, Dusoum Khyenpa (1110–93), instituted the political–religious system of the rebirth of the great spiritual masters (*tulkou*). This method of succession has always sparked debate about the authenticity of the reincarnations, because the successor is identified at a very young age. One of the regents of the current Karmapa contests the authority given to the young man who holds the title, for this very reason.

The current Karmapa, recently defected

Ugyen Trinley Dorje was born in Eastern Tibet on 26 June 1985, enthroned as the 17th Karmapa in 1992, and fled from his monastery in Tsurphu (60 kilometres (37 miles) from Lhasa) at the age of fourteen. Accompanied by his sister (a nun) and two monks, he reached Dharamsala in India on 5 January 2000, where he was welcomed by the Dalai Lama. Acknowledged by both the Chinese authorities and the Dalai Lama (an unusual occurrence), Dorje, who did not want to be used as a political pawn, could have been a major trump card for propagandists in the Chinese government. While he resided in Tibet he embodied 'the expression of religious freedom' and thus to the occupying Chinese, he diminished the predominant role 'of the reactionary band whose leader was a dangerous separatist, the Dalai Lama.' His defection embarrassed China, while Tibetans in exile see new hope in the figure of the 17th Karmapa.

Buddhist luminaries in Western Europe

Several 20th-century Europeans undertook explorations of the ever-mysterious Orient. The writings of Alexandra David-Neel in the 1930s, and the documentaries and accounts by Arnaud Desjardin, hint at the great spirituality of the Tibetan masters. The arrival of Zen and Tibetan masters in the West initiated more direct encounters, and their teachings took root in Europe. Here are some descriptions of a few of the more notable personalities of relatively recent years.

Kalu Rinpoche

Born in 1905 in the Eastern Tibetan province of Kham, Kalu Rinpoche is considered to be one of the greatest contemporary Tibetan spiritual masters, and one of the most influential guides in the West, due in no small part to his generosity and captivating charisma. He visited France for the first time in 1971 and founded several centres over the years, notably in Burgundy, Normandy and Dauphiné. To transmit his knowledge, he trained French teachers among them the Lama Denis Teundroup and the Lama Tcheuky. In the 1980s, he brought together Tibetan and Western scholars to translate the fundamental Buddhist texts. He visited the UK in 1987, where he gave lectures at several Buddhist centres, including the Samye Ling Tibetan monastery in Eskdalemuir, south-west Scotland. Kalu Rinpoche died peacefully on 10 May 1989, seated in the meditation position. Recognised by the Dalai Lama on 17 September 1990, the new incarnation of Kalu Rinpoche was born in the body of his faithful nephew's son, Lama Gyaltsen. When he is not travelling, the child studies and resides in the Sonada monastery, near Darjeeling in Western Bengal.

Dagpo Rinpoche

Born in 1932 in the Kongpo region, south-east of Lhasa, Dagpo Rinpoche fled Tibet during the Chinese invasion and has lived in Paris since 1960. This exceptional man taught his mother tongue at INALCO (the French National Institute of Oriental Languages and Civilisations) from 1963 until his retirement in 1992. When he was just one year old, he was recognised by the 13th Dalai Lama as the reincarnation of a great master (*tulkou*). The current Dalai Lama has encouraged Dagpo Rinpoche to teach. He founded a Buddhist congregation and the Institut Guepele cultural association in Veneux-les-Sablons, where retreats and study sessions take place. A Doctor of Philosophy, Rinpoche is of the Gelugpa lineage and teaches in Bordeaux, the Netherlands, Indonesia and Malaysia. He has visited the UK on at least one occasion. In 1998, he wrote an autobiography of his quiet but illuminating path in life (see Bibliography).

Sogyal Rinpoche

Born in 1947, this Tibetan disciple of great Buddhist masters studied at the universities of Delhi and Cambridge and has taught in the West since 1974. His communication skills took him to America, Europe, Australia and Asia to meet a great number of students. He founded the Rigpa centres, which can be found virtually anywhere in the world. His understanding of Western psychology has enabled him to communicate Buddhist ideas successfully, while his direct style, his participation as an actor in the film *Little Buddha* and his book *The Tibetan Book of Living and Dying* (translated into a dozen or so languages) have provided him with a large audience. Sogyal Rinpoche considers his purpose in life to be to bring Buddhist teaching to the West.

Deshimaru Taisen

The arrival of this Japanese master in Paris in 1967 contributed in great measure to the introduction of Zen to France. His knowledge of Christianity and Western thought prompted him to liken the Rule of Saint Benedict to Zen. He created hundreds of Zen study centres and founded the Association Zen Internationale in Paris (with a chapter in the UK). A descendant of a samurai family, he preached the Zen experience right up until his death on 30 April 1982. His many writings encouraged his disciples to follow in his footsteps.

D. T. Suzuki (1870–1966)

This Japanese Buddhist scholar is known as one of the greatest modern interpreters of Zen in the West. He did an enormous amount to arouse interest in Zen. He was a lay student of Master Shaku Soen from the Engaju Temple in Kamakura, Japan, where he followed Zen training focusing primarily on the intellectual interpretation of Zen teachings. He wrote 20 works in English on Zen Buddhism, attempting to explain its nature and its role in the Western world.

Christmas Humphreys (1901–83)

This prominent English Buddhist adopted Buddhism as a way of life in 1918, and attended Buddhist lectures in 1923. Along with Aileen Faulkner, who later became his wife, he founded the Buddhist Lodge of the Theosophical Society in 1924, which became the Buddhist Society in 1926. He was the publisher of the respected journal *The Middle Way* and was Vice-President of the World Fellowship of Buddhists.

Buddhist art

Like all humanity's great spiritual traditions, Buddhism has made full use of the talents of its artists, sculptors, painters and architects.

Buddhist artistic imagery

Since Buddhist art is constrained by strict rules, it is often formal, transmitting a strong spiritual power over and above its purely aesthetic beauty. Its aim is to recall the ideals of the doctrine, and the different representations all share the same goal: to put people into contact with the energy of the Buddha and of beings moving towards Enlightenment. Buddhist inspiration, closely interwoven with the tradition of the Divine Tao in China, Korea and Japan, involves full communion with nature; an empathy towards the plant and animal world is felt in some works. The true essence of beings becomes manifest in the realm of shapes. Indo-Greek and Persian as well as Indian, Chinese, Khmer, Tibetan, Korean and Mongolian artists influenced Buddhist imagery. Buddhist art masterpieces fulfil both spiritual and cultural roles.

Zanabazar – prince and sculptor (1635–1723)

Leaving aside Zanabazar's qualities as an astute diplomat and renowned novelist, he was also an exceptional sculptor. The refined art of this descendant of Genghis Khan sheds magnificent light on the complexity of the Tantric Buddhist iconography. After visiting Lhasa to study with the fifth Dalai Lama and the Panchen Lama, he was acknowledged as the reincarnation of a famous Tibetan scholar, Taranatha. Parallel to his monastic activities, he ran a casting workshop and sculpted his own statues of the postures codified in the Buddhist Vajrayana canon. His gilded bronzes with polychrome highlights won him great artistic acclaim. The delicate poses and expressive faces of his statues convey the great spirituality of Mongolian art.

The ninth reincarnation of Zanabazar now lives in Dharamsala, not far from the current residence of the Dalai Lama, where he studies and teaches Buddhist precepts.

The Bamiyan statues

Overlooking the Bamiyan Valley, in the heart of the Hindu Kush in Afghanistan, long-departed sculptors carved some of Asia's most impressive statues into the cliff-face, several hundred years ago. In more peaceful times they were a tourist attraction, and it had been hoped that Afghanistan's ruling Taleban party would preserve them for less puritanical times, but in March 2001 the Taleban set about destroying them, using whatever weapons were to hand, form anti-tank guns to spades. They claimed the statues were idolatrous and contrary to Islamic doctrine, and their destruction was part of a wave of icon-smashing which also saw some of the non-Islamic treasures in the National Museum in Kabul being destroyed. The two largest statues were 53 and 38 metres high. The former was for many centuries the largest representation of the Buddha anywhere in the world. In earlier times they were painted and dressed in gargantuan robes, and rich frescoes adorned the walls. What was the importance of Bamiyan, that these imposing statues were created here? It lies on the Old Silk Road along which traders travelled between the Roman Empire and China and India. Now, the interaction of different cultures that contributed to the richness of the site has proved its downfall, as one ideology rejects and destroys the legacy of another.

Sculpture of Zanabazar dating from the late 17th century or early 18th century. This is kept in the Choijin-lama monastery (Museum of the History of Religion), in Ulan Bator, Mongolia.

Museums in Britain with significant Buddhist collections

There are no UK museums specifically dedicated to Buddhism, but the following museums house important collections.

The British Museum, London

This museum houses the largest collection of Buddhist artefacts and artworks in the UK. Using the database on the Museum's website, it is possible to view the 160+ Buddhist items on display.

The Buddhist objects from India and Pakistan include first to third-century bas-relief stone carvings of the birth and death of the Buddha, and the veneration of a stupa; first- and second-century gold and bronze reliquaries and coins; bodhisattva amulets; and stone second- to fifth-century seated and standing statues of Siddharta. The Sri Lankan objects include a statue of Tara, the consort of Avalokitesavara, and an 18th-century, gilt, bronze and silver statue of the Buddha. From Thailand there is a 14th-century bronze figure of a walking Buddha, and, from Indonesia, a tenth-century bronze Tantric Buddhist image of Vairocana.

Tibet is well represented by 18th- and 19th-century paintings of arhats and Buddhist guardians, bronze figures of a Buddhist saint and a Bon deity, a copper alloy statue of Tara, a gilt–bronze image of Padmasambhava, a prayer stone with carved mantras, a clay figure of a female deity, two ceremonial trumpets, a portable shrine, and a prayer wheel. Notable objects from Nepal include a 12th–13th-century stone bas-relief depicting Hindu/Buddhist myths and a 15th-century bronze figure of a bodhisattva.

There are several Chinese ninth–tenth-century embroidered silk hangings and paintings depicting the life of Siddharta, the bodhisattva Avalokitesvara and the buddha Maitreya, as well as two 14th-century hanging scroll paintings of arhats, and a 14th-century stoneware figure of a Buddhist monk.

The Korean Foundation Gallery in the North Wing features a colossal Buddhist sculpture never before seen outside Korea. There are also 12th-century ritual objects, such as tea bowls and a water sprinkler, a 14th-century scroll painting of Avalokitesvara and some 18th-century paintings of scenes from the life of the Buddha.

The collection's particular strength is its Japanese section, including rare minature wooden stupas from the 8th century; 11th- and 12th-century images of Buddhist deities, 12th-century paper scrolls featuring calligraphy and bodhisattvas; a 13th-century mask of a bodhisattva; and 14th-century hanging scroll paintings of Buddhist deities, the death of the Buddha, Buddha's disciples, the monk Jion Daishi, bodhisattvas and a mandala. Other objects include a 15th-century bronze figure of a bodhisattva, a 17th century bronze statue of Siddharta, and 16th–19th-century hanging scroll paintings depicting subjects as diverse as Amithaba, Bodhidharma, the life of Siddharta, Zen calligraphy and the realms of Buddhist hell.

The Victoria and Albert Museum, London

This museum is the largest and most influential museum of decorative arts in the world. There are a number of Buddhist items on display, with several hundred more in storage. Stored items can be viewed by special arrangement. The collection features items from most Buddhist countries, particularly China and India, including textile hangings, ritual objects, paintings, some notable Chinese Buddhist sculptures, and objects connected with the Japanese tea ceremony.

The Ashmolean Museum of Art and Archaeology, Oxford

The Ashmolean has over a hundred Buddhist items on display, covering all the Buddhist countries, although the majority are from India, Tibet and Nepal. The collection's particular strengths are images of the Buddha and the bodhisattvas, as well as Buddhist paintings.

14th-century statue of a mendicant and another image of Amithaba, this time from the 16th century. Tibetan Buddhism is represented by a 16th-century gilt–copper statue of a monk and a 17th-century gilt–bronze garuda.

The British Library has a large number of Buddhist books and manuscripts in its Oriental and India office collections, including the world's oldest printed material – a set of Buddhist sutras.

Buddhist artefacts can also be found in the collections of the following museums (see the Address section of this book)

Birmingham City Museum and Art Gallery
Durham University Oriental Museum
The Manchester Museum (University of Manchester)
The Royal Museum of Scotland

The Museum of East Asian Art, Bath

This museum, which was founded by the collector Brian McElney, has a number of Buddhist artefacts in its collections from China, Japan, Korea and Southeast Asia, including a Chinese stone head of the buddha Amithaba and a marble figure of Avalokitesvara (the most popular Buddhist deity), both dating from the sixth century. There are several younger Chinese statues in gilt–bronze, including a

European museums

Guimet, the French National Museum of Asian Arts

The Musée Guimet, one of the world's most prestigious oriental art museums, with its collection of over 45,000 artefacts and 110,000 works of art, has now reopened after four years of renovation work. It is the largest museum of Buddhist art in Europe. There is a new, purpose-built, well-signposted site to provide the perfect setting for the jewels of Buddhist art. Follow the guide ...

A little history

Initially, the Musée Guimet was conceived as a museum of the history of religion, dedicated to furthering the understanding of Eastern civilisations. It was founded by Emile Guimet, a wealthy manufacturer from Lyons. In 1876, he visited Japan, bringing back a large number of Buddhist objects. He moved to Paris in 1888, where he ordered the construction of the building that houses the present-day museum. After his death in 1918, the museum's Asian credentials became progressively established, especially between the two World Wars, when it housed the collection of the Musée Indochinois du Trocadéro. In 1928, it became a national museum and inherited some remarkable pieces of Afghan art. In 1945, the Far East collections of the Louvre were also transferred to the museum. Since then, a well-planned acquisitions policy, which has benefited from legacies and donations, has continued to enrich this showcase for Buddhist art.

The restoration

The museum was closed to the public for four years. Its complete renovation was supervised by the architect Henri Gaudin, and the presentation chosen by the curator marries the fresh architectural space with a new tour through the exhibits. The reconstruction gives a clearer, more palpable understanding of how Buddhism spread through the various Asian countries. In addition to the permanent collection, there are photography archives and a library that holds a number of precious works devoted to Buddhism, including the Tibetan library that Alexandra David-Neel bequeathed to the museum, as well as an extensive collection of periodicals (in French, English, Chinese, Tibetan and Japanese). Visits, teaching and documentation are available in English.

Works depicting the Buddhist pantheon

The annexe to the Musée Guimet at 19 Place d'Iéna, and the gallery at 59 Avenue Foch, house the collections of the Buddhist Pantheon of China and Japan. Several hundred Japanese works, depicting the proliferation of the Buddhist faith, are on display, as well as masterpieces of Chinese Buddhist art.

The Rijksmuseum, Amsterdam

This is the national museum of the Netherlands. It has a small but significant collection of Indonesian, Chinese, Japanese and Indian Buddhist objects in its Asian Art rooms, including fine statues from Japan and China.

The Metropolitan Museum, New York

The Asian art collection at the Metropolitan Museum in New York is the largest and most comprehensive in the West. Each of the many civilisations of Asia is represented by outstanding works that provide an unrivalled experience of the artistic traditions of nearly half the world. The collection of more than 60,000 objects includes paintings, prints, calligraphy, sculptures, metalwork, ceramics, lacquers, works of decorative art and textiles, from East Asia, South Asia, the Himalayan kingdoms and Southeast Asia.

The Museum has been collecting Asian art since the late 19th century. The Department of Far Eastern art was established in 1915. In 1988 a new wing was built to house the huge number of exhibits. Many pieces in the Metropolitan's collection reveal the similarities in form and iconography occasioned by a shared Buddhist heritage. The Charlotte W. Weber galleries hold a notable collection of Chinese monumental stone sculptures, including rare Buddhist images from the Tang to the Ming dynasties. The Arts of Japan galleries, in the Sackler Wing, include an altar platform for the display of Buddhist sculptures, modelled on a 12th-century example. The galleries for the Arts of South and Southeast Asia represent the visual traditions of India, Afghanistan, Pakistan, Bangladesh, Burma (Myanmar), Cambodia, Thailand, Vietnam and Indonesia. Areas of particular strength include Buddhist stone and bronze sculptures from the Kushan dynasty (first to third century AD), Kashmiri and Pala period sculptures (ninth to 13th century), an unparalleled collection of early South-east Asian metalwork, and metal sculptures from the Khmer empire in Cambodia and Thailand (ninth to 14th century). Nepalese and Tibetan religious imagery from the eighth through to the 19th century is exhibited in three additional galleries on the third floor.

An Arts of Korea Gallery was opened in 1998. Objects from the Museum's permanent collection, especially Buddhist paintings and ceramics of the Koryo (fourth to tenth century) and Choson (tenth to 14th century) dynasties, together with thematic exhibitions featuring loans from collections in the US and abroad, provide a comprehensive overview of Korea's artistic and cultural heritage. The importance of Buddhism in daily life and its pervasive influence as a creative and spiritual force in early Korean society are seen, for example, in silver-inlaid incense burners and vessels, as well as in bronze bells and gongs made for use in temples. Among the monuments of Buddhist art is a large gilt–bronze image of the buddha Maitreya, from the late sixth century, whose contemplative expression epitomises the powerful presence of Korean Buddhist sculpture. Portable shrines and reliquaries exquisitely crafted in gilt–bronze are evidence of the increasingly personal expression of Buddhist devotion in the Koryo dynasty. There are also some exquisite fourteenth-century hanging scroll paintings, and a folding book of similar age. with elegant calligraphy and a frontispiece depicting popular tales from the Lotus Sutra.

The National Gallery of Australia

The building contains a number of sculptures and paintings from most Buddhist countries. From India, there are some exquisite tenth-century metalwork images of the Buddha, and a 12th-century image of the goddess Prajnaparamita, the personification of the Buddhist sutra of the same name. Early sculptures from Pakistan (formerly northern India) include a first–third-century stone garuda and a stone head of a disciple, both of which show the distinctive influence of Greek classicism, as does another stone head of the Buddha. Also from Pakistan, there is an eighth-century bronze image of Avaloskitesvara, the young bodhisattva of compassion, in standing pose, with twelve arms either carrying symbolic objects or forming gestures of reassurance, charity and adoration, as well as his main attribute of compassion.

The Thai artefacts include an unusually slender 18th-century depiction of the Buddha, wearing a cape, pointed cap and ornate jewellery. There is also a 14th–16th-century statue of the Buddha – seated on a lotus pedestal – summoning the goddess of the earth. Burma is represented by two 19th-century lacquered sculptures of Buddha, again calling the earth to witness – a favourite theme. There are also two 19th-century gilt and lacquered wood figures of his disciples and an early 20th-century religious hanging depicting scenes from the Buddha's life. From Nepal, there is a 13th-century image of Avalokitesvara, holding out his right hand in the gesture of discourse (vitarka mudra). From China there is a 15th-century metal-work image of the bodhisattva Padmapani, which shows distinct Indian influences – the body is decorated with

ornate jewellery and organic forms. A seventh–eighth-century Chinese tile depicts a Buddhist guardian figure, thought to ward off evil spirits from Buddhist temples. Japanese Buddhism is represented by a beautiful 14th-century wooden sculpture of a Japanese prince praying to the Buddha, a painting depicting two bodhisattva figures and the sixteen protectors of the Buddha, and a 19th-century line painting by the famous Zen artist, Sengai.

Alexandra David-Neel – Buddhist scholar and author

Born in Paris in 1868, Alexandra David-Neel's name has become inextricably linked with the country to which she was most drawn, Tibet. A formidably determined traveller, at a time when journeying abroad was generally far less common, less easy, and certainly more difficult for women than it is today, she was to become the first European woman to enter the holy city of Lhasa.

Despite her English-sounding name, Alexandra was French, and as a young woman in Paris attended lectures on eastern religions that kindled her desire to travel to and learn more about Asia. Fulfilling some of these early dreams, she travelled to India, Ceylon and the Middle and Far East, and in 1904 married Philippe Francois Neel in Tunis. They did not live together long, but despite their early separation, Philippe was to finance many of her travels. In 1911, Alexandra left for Northern India where she became the first Western woman to interview the Dalai Lama. This meeting fired her determination to learn more about Tibetan Buddhism, but the Tibetans had closed their borders and so, when she was ready to make her first visit to Tibet in 1914, she was forced to slip across the border illegally. Spending several months in a monastery, she studied Buddhist teachings before moving back into the Northern Indian region of Sikkim where she spent several more months living a hermit-like existence in a cave. It was in Sikkim that she met Yongden, a monk

whom she was to later adopt as her son and who would accompany her faithfully until his death in 1955.

Alexandra continued her studies, immersing herself in Buddhist culture, and, after a second sortie into Tibet, began to dream of penetrating to the heart of the country. Since the British had begun to bar access from India, this time she decided to enter via the more circuitous route of China, travelling through Burma, Korea and Japan, reaching Peking in 1917. From Peking, she crossed China with Yongden at her side to enter Tibet once more. They stayed in the monastery of Kumbum for several years. Finally, in 1923 Yongden and Alexandra set out on foot for Lhasa disguised as Tibetan beggars, Alexandra's face darkened and her hair dyed black. The journey was extremely arduous and perilous. They were at considerable risk from bandits and discovery by the authorities, but finally reached the forbidden city in October and lived there as pilgrims, undetected for two months.

In 1925, fourteen years after leaving France, Alexandra returned to find that her exploits had made her famous. She was feted and showered with honours, being made a Chevalier of the Legion of Honour and awarded the Gold Medal of the Geographical Society of France. True to her indomitable spirit, Alexandra finally died at the age of 100 in 1969. Her most audacious Tibetan journey is related in her book *My Journey to Lhasa* (see Further reading).

Buddhist cuisine

Being a Buddhist doesn't mean that you have to be a vegetarian. At least, the first Buddhists were not vegetarian. However, over the centuries and with the geographical expansion of Buddhism, things have changed considerably. Each country has kept its own culinary traditions, to which Buddhism has added a particular colouring. Such is the case in Japan, where several centuries of Zen Buddhism have lent the cuisine an ever-increasing sobriety, or in Tibet, where the culture is characterised by the traditions of mountain life.

In Japan

'Do not leave washing the rice or preparing the vegetables to others but use your own hands, your own eyes, your own sincerity. Do not fragment your attention but see what each moment calls for; if you take care of just one thing then you will be careless of the other. Do not miss the opportunity of offering even a single drop into the ocean of merit or of adding a single grain to the mountain of beneficial activity. The Zen Monastic Rules state that "If the Six Flavours (bitter, sour, sweet, hot, mild, salty) are not in harmony and the three virtues (light, clean, dignified) are lacking, then the Tenzo [head cook] is not truly serving the community." Be careful of sand when you wash the rice, be careful of the rice when you throw out the sand. Take care all the time and the three virtues will be naturally complete and the six flavours harmonious.' This excerpt – which can be found in *Cooking Zen*, Great Matter Publications, 1996 – is taken from the *Eihei Shingi* anthology, written by

Dogen in 1237 and dedicated to the 'future generations of sages who will study the way'. Dogen was a Buddhist thinker and monk who founded the Japanese Soto, which considers seated meditation (*zazen*) to be central to its practice.

In Tibet

According to the Buddha, 'It is not through the partaking of meat or fish that a man becomes impure, but through drunkenness, obstinacy, bigotry, deceit, envy, self-exaltation, disparagement of others and evil intentions – through these a man becomes impure.' While opposed to all acts of killing, even those committed by animals for food, the Buddha never strictly prohibited the consumption of meat or fish. As a matter of survival, meat and dairy products are the two staples of the Tibetan diet, and monks and nuns accept the meat products that the nomad pastors give them. Vegetarians are rare in the high Tibetan plateaux.

Dogen, monk and famous thinker, lived in Japan in the 13th century.

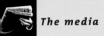

Buddhism – a concept that sells

The current European fad for Buddhism has not escaped the attention of journalists and advertising companies. Below are some examples of the trend.

For the last few years, newspaper headlines have contained a surprising number of Buddhist references. The context was initially sociological, then cultural, and finally religious, but the phenomenon has even spread into the fashion, design and cooking sections of glossy magazines and newspaper supplements.

From editorials to advertising, communications gurus tread the lines between exoticism, wisdom and mockery. 'Zen' and Buddhist priests are used to sell air travel, cars, energy, furniture, insecticides, radios, and even dog food. What are we to make of this? The Japanese Zen monk, painter, calligrapher and poet, Sengai (1750–1837) may just have provided us with an answer ahead of his time:

We think of many things
Of this and that
But the spirit, the Buddha and living beings
Are all three without differentiation.
(**Gibbon Sengaï**, *Traces d'encre*, (Ink Marks), 1994 Paris)

'That was Zen, this is now.'

(19 Dec 1999, *The Guardian*)

'Battle of the Lamas.'

(4 March 2000, *The Daily Telegraph*)

'Zen and the art of movie making.'

(13 April 2000, *Time*)

'Honk if you love Buddha.'

(12 June 2000, *New York Times*)

'The Dalai Lama – beyond the fad.'

(*Washington Post*)

'Buddhism nears mainstream in US.'

(29 Jan 2000, *New York Times*)

'Political notoriety puts light on
Buddhist trend.'
(29 April 2000, *New York Times*)

'Life after God.'
(20 April 1999, *The Guardian*)

'A case of
greed or bad
karma?'
(26 March 1999,
The Guardian)

'A message of hope; appeal of
Buddhism grows in US.'
(14 April 2000, *New York Times*)

Films

LIGHT OF ASIA
(PREM SANYAS OR DIE LEUCHTE ASIENS)
by **Franz Osten and Rai Himansu,**
Indo-Austrian, 1925.
This silent Indian film details the life and childhood of Siddharta Gautama. A true gem for cinema-buffs.

LOST HORIZON
by **Franck Capra,**
United States, 1937.
Adapted from James Hilton's 1933 novel. A plane crashes in the heart of the snow-capped Himalayas. The passengers arrive at a lamasery located in Shangri-La, an isolated paradise where peace and abundance reign.

BUDDHA
(SHAKA)
by **Misumi Kenji,**
Japan, 1961.
The first Japanese film in 70 mm recounts the life story of the Buddha Gautama.

SIDDARTHA
by **Conrad Rooks,**
adapted from the novel by Hermann Hesse, Indo-American, 1973.
A man questioning existence encounters the Buddhist doctrine and his life leads him along other paths.

MANDALA (*MANDARA*)
by **Im Kwon-Taek,**
Korea, 1983.
A sceptical monk questions the Buddha's doctrine and begins a life of wandering with another degenerate monk and an omnipresent bottle of alcohol. Friendship and conflict, with a background critique of religion.

WHY HAS BODHIDHARMA LEFT FOR THE EAST?
(TALMAGATONGTCHOGU RO KAN KADALGUN?)
by **Bae Yonh-Kyun,**
Korea, 1989.
Peaceful and dynamic meditation on Buddhism. In a tiny hermitage, an ageing monk detaches himself from life. He is tormented by the fact that he has abandoned his family and by a melancholy, orphaned boy monk.

LITTLE BUDDHA
by **Bernardo Bertolucci,**
Franco-American, 1993.
Tibetan monks in search of their departed master see the emanation of their eminent spiritual leader in a Western child. The life of Siddharta Gautama told in the form of a children's fable.

SEVEN YEARS IN TIBET
by **Jean-Jacques Annaud,**
United States, 1997.
According to the director, this cinematographic adaptation of the story of the Nazi mountaineer Heinrich Harrer describes 'the redemption of a man who loses himself physically in order to find his soul.'

KUNDUN
by **Martin Scorsese,**
United States, 1998.
More evocative than historical, this is a biography of the 14th Dalai Lama's early years and the Chinese invasion.

HIMALAYA
(HIMALAYA, L'ENFANCE D'UN CHEF)
by **Eric Valli,**
France, 1999.
In a lost village in the Dolpo region, in the north-west Nepalese Himalayas, an old chief refuses to let his young rival lead a large caravan of yaks.

THE CUP
(PHÖRPA)
by **Norbu Khyentse,**
Bhutan, 1999.
This first full-length film directed by a Bhutanese Lama is a humorous tale of the life of young football-mad monks, told in Tibetan. While two young Tibetans flee their native land and discover monastic life, one mischievous young monk has thoughts only for the World Cup ...

FRANCIS BOUYGUES et JEREMY THOMAS
présentent

UN FILM DE BERNARDO BERTOLUCCI
LITTLE BUDDHA

"LITTLE BUDDHA"   KEANU REEVES   YING RUOCHENG   CHRIS ISAAK   ALEX WIESENDANGER et BRIDGET FONDA

décors et costumes par JAMES ACHESON   montage PIETRO SCALIA   photo VITTORIO STORARO AIC·A.S.C.   musique composée et dirigée par RYUICHI SAKAMOTO

sujet original de BERNARDO BERTOLUCCI   scénario RUDY WURLITZER et MARK PEPLOE   producteur JEREMY THOMAS   réalisé par BERNARDO BERTOLUCCI

Zen and the koan

In the Zen Buddhist tradition, a *koan* is an enigmatic or paradoxical phrase to aid you on your way to Enlightenment – like a riddle that cannot be solved by pure reason alone.

Two monks were arguing about the temple flag waving in the wind. One said, 'The flag moves.' The other said, 'The wind moves.' Their Master said, 'Gentlemen! It is not the flag that moves. It is not the wind that moves. It is your mind that moves.'

A philosopher asked the Buddha, 'Without words, without silence, will you tell me the truth?' The Buddha sat quietly. The philosopher then bowed and thanked the Buddha, saying, 'With your loving kindness I have cleared away my delusions and entered the true path.' After the philosopher had gone, Ananda asked the Buddha what the philosopher had attained. The Buddha commented, 'A good horse runs even at the shadow of a whip.'

A monk said to Joshu, 'I have just entered this monastery. Please teach me.' 'Have you eaten your breakfast?' Joshu asked. 'Yes, I have,' replied the student. 'Then you had better wash your bowl.'

One day the governor of Kyoto came to call upon Keichu. He handed the attendant a card that said, Kitagaki, Governor of Kyoto. Upon receiving the card, Keichu told the attendant that he had no interest in seeing such a person. When the attendant brought back the card with apologies, Kitagaki said, 'That was my mistake,' and scratched out the words 'Governor of Kyoto.' 'Ah,' said Keichu, when he saw the card again. 'I want to see Kitagaki.'

The man looked at the flower, the flower smiled.

Question to a Master:
'Are you in your heart?'
His answer: 'No, I am in my heart.'

What is the sound of one hand clapping?

What is your original face before your mother and father are born?

Nan-in, a Japanese master, received a university professor who came to inquire about Zen. Nan-in served tea. He poured his visitor's cup full, and then kept on pouring. The professor watched the overflow until he no longer could restrain himself. 'It is overfull. No more will go in!' 'Like this cup,' Nan-in said, 'you are full of your own opinions and speculations. How can I show you Zen unless you first empty your cup?'

Te-shan was sitting outside doing zazen. Lung-t'an asked him why he didn't go home. Te-shan answered, 'Because it's dark.' Lung-t'an then lit a candle and handed it to him. As Te-shan was about to take it, Lung-t'an blew it out. Te-shan is enlightened and bows.

'What is Zen?' asked a monk.
'Brick and stone', responded Shih-t'ou.
'What is the Tao?'
'A block of wood.'

Information at a glance

▼

ORGANISATIONS CONNECTED WITH BUDDHISM

THE BUDDHIST SOCIETY
58 Eccleston Square, London
SW1V 1PH
Tel: 020 7834 5858
Fax: 020 7976 5238
http://www.buddsoc.org.uk
Publishes books on
Buddhism and related
subjects

ARUNA RATANAGIRI MONASTERY
Harnham, Belsey
Northumberland NE20 0HF
Tel: 01661 881 612
Fax: 01661 881 019
Email: community@
ratanagiri.org.uk
Representative Buddhist
monastery in the UK.

INTERNATIONAL ZEN ASSOCIATION, UK
For information,
Tel: 0117 942 4347 (Bristol)
http://www.zen-azi.org

AUCKLAND BUDDHIST CENTRE
Friends of the Western
Buddhist Order
381 Richmond Rd.
Grey Lynn
Auckland
New Zealand
Tel: 00 64 9 378 1120
Fax: 00 64 9 378 1226
Email:
auckbudcen@xtra.co.nz
Website:
http://www.mysite.xtra.co.
nz/~auckbudcen

AUCKLAND SHAMBHALA CENTRE
Contact: Dan Dlugose
Tel: 00 64 9 575 7899
Email:
dlugose@lycosmail.com

Website:
http://www.shambhala.
org/center/auckland
Wellington contact: Ms
Marian Bond
Tel: 00 64 4 475 9223
Email: colin.pratt@xtra.co.nz
(Vajrayana)

MAGAZINES

TRICYCLE
A non-profit-making
quarterly founded in 1991,
with an educational charter
to spread the dharma
http://www.tricycle.com

INTERNET

BUDDHIST INFORMATION NETWORK
http://www.buddhanet.net
A non-profit-making
organization affiliated with
the Buddha Dharma
Education Association Inc.

'Buddhism in Australia – a
Bibliography' is an Internet
resource compiled by
Michelle Spuler of the
Religion Department of
Colorado College, USA.
http://www.spuler.org/ms/
biblio.htm

The Australian Buddhist
Directory can be downloaded
as a pdf file from
http://www.buddhanet.
net/baorgs.htm

PORTAL TO MAIN TIBETAN BUDDHISM SITES
http://www.tibet.org

TIBET INFORMATION SITE
Recent press releases, lists of
Buddhist centres, the life of
the Dalai Lama, etc.
http://www.tibet.co.uk

Buddhist art

▼

MUSEUMS AND LIBRARIES IN THE UK

ASHMOLEAN MUSEUM OF ART AND ARCHAEOLOGY, OXFORD
Beaumont Street
Oxford OX1 2PH
Tel: 01865 278000
Website: http://www.
ashmol.ox.ac.uk

BIRMINGHAM MUSEUM AND ART GALLERY
Chamberlain Square,
Birmingham B3 3DH
Tel: 0121 303 1966
Website: http://www.
birmingham.gov.uk/bmag

BRITISH LIBRARY
Oriental and India Office
Collections
96 Euston Road
London NW1 2DB
Tel: 020 7412 7873
Fax: 020 7412 7641
Email: oioc-enquiries@bl.uk
Website: http://portico.bl.uk

BRITISH MUSEUM, LONDON,
Great Russell Street
London WC1B 3DG
Tel: 020 7636 1555
Website: http://www.
thebritishmuseum.ac.uk

DURHAM UNIVERSITY ORIENTAL MUSEUM,
Elvet Hill
Durham City DH1 3TH
Tel: 0191 374 2911
Email: oriental.museum@
dur.ac.uk

MUSEUM OF EAST ASIAN ART
12 Bennett Street
Bath BA1 2QL
Tel: 01225 46 4640
Fax: 01225 46 1718
http://www.east-asian-
art.co.uk

ROYAL MUSEUM OF SCOTLAND
National Museums of
Scotland
Chambers Street
Edinburgh EH1 1JF
Tel: 0131 225 7534
Fax: 0131 220 4819
Website: http://www.
nms.ac.uk/royal/

THE MANCHESTER MUSEUM
The University of Manchester
Oxford Road
Manchester M13 9PL
Tel: 0161 275 2634
Fax: 0161 275 2676
Website: http://
museum.man.ac.uk

THE VICTORIA AND ALBERT MUSEUM
Cromwell Road
South Kensington
London SW7 2RL
Tel: 020 7942 2000
Fax: 020 7942 2266
Website: http://
www.vam.ac.uk

MUSEUMS IN EUROPE

FRENCH NATIONAL MUSEUM OF ASIAN ARTS – MUSÉE GUIMET
Largest Buddhist collection
in Europe. Reopened in
2000 after extensive
renovation (see page 107).
6 Place d'Iéna, 75116, Paris
Tel: 00 331 47 23 61 65
Fax: 00 331 47 20 57 50
http://www.museeguimet.
fr

MUSEUM OF EAST ASIAN ART
Universitatsstr 100
50674 Köln
Germany
Tel: 00 49 221 9405180
Fax: 00 49 221 407290

RIJKSMUSEUM,
Stadhouderskade 42
Amsterdam
Tel: 00 31 20 6747 077
Fax: 00 31 20 6747 001
Email:
info@rijksmuseum.nl
Website:
http://www.rijksmuseum.
org/

THE UNITED STATES

THE METROPOLITAN MUSEUM OF ART, NEW YORK
1000 Fifth Avenue at 82nd Street
New York NY10028-0198
Tel: 00 1 212 535 7710
Website: http://www.
metmuseum.org
The largest collection of Asian artefacts in the West.

MUSEUMS AND GALLERIES IN AUSTRALIA

NATIONAL GALLERY OF AUSTRALIA,
Parkes Place
Parkes, ACT
Tel: 00 61 2 6240 6502
Fax: 00 61 2 6240 6529
Website:
http://www.nga.gov.au

ASIAN ART IN LONDON

A major international event, now enjoying its third consecutive year, in which leading London Asian art dealers, major auction houses and academic institutions come together to demonstrate London's pre-eminence in the world of Asian art.

32 Dover Street, Mayfair,
London W1S 4NE
Tel: 020 7499 2215
Fax: 020 7499 2216
http://www.
asianartinlondon.com

OTHERS

ARTS OF ASIA
Foremost International Asian Arts and Antiques Magazine
http://www.
artsofasianet.com

His Holiness the Dalai Lama, *The Dalai Lama's Book of Wisdom*, Thorsons Publishing, 2000.
Alexandra David-Neel, *My Journey to Lhasa*, first published 1927, by Heinemann, republished by Virago, 1986.
Alexandra David-Neel, *Magic and Mystery in Tibet*, Dover Publications, 1986.
Dogen, *Cooking Zen: Zen Master Dogen's Instructions to the Kitchen Master and On How to Use Your Bowls*, translated by Ven. Anzan Hoshin sensei and Yasuda Joshu roshi, Great Matter Publications, 1996.
Erich Fromm, *Zen Buddhism Psychoanalysis*, Souvenir Press, 1974.
Sunniva Harte, *Zen Gardening*, Stewart Tabori and Chong, 1999.
Peter Harvey, *An Introduction to Buddhism*, Cambridge University Press, 1990.
Christmas Humphreys, *A Popular Dictionary of Buddhism*, NTC Publishing Group, 1997.
Eva Judy Jansen, *Book of Buddhas: Ritual Symbolism used on Buddhist Statuary and Ritual Objects*, Samuel Weiser, 1993.
Kenneth Kushner, *One Arrow, One Life: Zen, Archery, Enlightenment*, Charles E. Tuttle, 2000.
Lionel Landry, *The Land and People of Burma*, J. B. Lippincott, 1968.
Peter Lorie and Julie Foarkes (compilers), *The Buddhist Directory*, Charles E. Tuttle, 1997.
Hermann Oldenberg, *Buddha – His Life, His Doctrine, His Order*, Pilgrim, 1998.
Orient Foundation (ed.), *A Handbook of Tibetan Culture: a Guide to Tibetan Centres and Resources Throughout the World*, Shambhala Publications, 1995.
Marco Polo, *The Travels*, translated with an Introduction by Ronald Latham, Penguin Classics, 1958.
Bokar Rinpoche *Meditation*, ClearPoint Press, 1993.
Kalu Rinpoche, *Excellent Buddhism: an Exemplary Life*, ClearPoint Press, 1995.
Sogyal Rinpoche, *The Tibetan Book of Living and Dying*, Harper, San Francisco, 1992.
Rolf. A. Stein, *Tibetan Civilisation*, translated from *La Civilisation tibetaine* by J. E. Stapleton Driver, Stanford, 1972.
Daisetz Teitaro Suzuki, Erich Fromm and Richard Martino, *Zen Buddhism and Psychoanalysis*, Souvenir Press, 1993.

Further reading

Edwin A. Burtt (ed.), *The Teachings of the Compassionate Buddha*, New American Library Trade, 2000.
Thomas Byrom (translator), *The Dhammapada: the Sayings of the Buddha*, Shambhala Publications, 1993.
Kate Crosby *et al.*, *A Concise Encyclopedia of Buddhism*, Oneworld Publications, 2000.
Paul Croucher, *Buddhism in Australia*, New South Wales University Press, 1989. *Key reference for Buddhism in Australia.*

Buddhist Art
Robert E. Fisher, *Art of Tibet (World of Art)*, Thames & Hudson, 1998.
David Jackson, *A History of Tibetan Painting: the Great Tibetan Painters and Their Traditions*, Wien, 1996.
Sarah K. Lukas (ed.), *The Art of Exile: Paintings by Tibetan Children in India*, Museum of New Mexico Press, 1997.
Pratapaditya Pal and Valrae Reynolds, *Art of the Himalayas: Treasures from Nepal and Tibet*, Hudson Hills Press, 1991.

ADIBOUDDHA
Term from the Vajrayana, designating an abstract entity, a supreme buddha, self-born, who created the universe.

AKSOBHYA
One of the five meditation buddhas. The Steadfast One.

AMIDISM
A philosophical movement that reveres the Buddha Amithaba ('Amida' in Japanese).

AMITHABA
One of the five meditation buddhas, the Boundless Light, later known as a buddha of Compassion.

AMOGASIDDHI
Another of the five meditation buddhas. The All-Accomplishing One.

APSARAS
Heavenly nymphs.

ARHAT
The perfected disciple. One who has completed the discipline of the Buddhist doctrine required to attain liberation.

ASCETICISM
Philosophy of self-denial, of not allowing oneself luxuries, often practised for religious reasons.

ASOKA
Emperor and founder of a unified India, he later converted to Buddhism and helped the religion to spread throughout his empire.

ASURA
One of the eight protectors of the Buddha.

AVALOKITESVARA
Popular Tibetan figure and protector. He is also a bodhisattva, an enlightened being of pure compassion, who is reincarnated in the Dalai Lama.

BACTRIA
Ancient country in Central Asia. It was one of the Hellenistic states founded by the successors of Alexander the Great. It was situated between the Hindu Kush mountains and the Oxus River.

BHIKKHU
Pali term for a monk or a Buddhist priest.

BODHI
Enlightenment, perfect understanding of the truth. Guiding state for knowledge of the ultimate nature of phenomena.

BODHIDHARMA
Monk who founded Chinese Buddhism in 520. Main theorist of the Mahayanist school of meditation.

BODHISATTVA
'Enlightened being' of pure compassion who has the spiritual capacity to reach buddhahood, but who chooses to be reincarnated in order to help others escape from the cycle of rebirth.

BODHI TREE
Pipal tree under which Siddharta Gautama achieved Enlightenment.

BON
Shamanistic Tibetan religion.

BOROBUDUR
Pyramidal monument – a mandala of stone – built in the eighth and ninth centuries in central Java.

BRAHMINISM
Indian (Hindu) religion that stems from Vedaism.

BRAHMINS
Elitist Indian priestly caste that held immense power during the lifetime of the historical Buddha.

BUDDHA
An epithet that refers either to Siddharta Gautama, the historical founder of Buddhism, or to a state of consciousness – the enlightenment produced by the opening of the mind, and qualifies all 'Enlightened' beings (Theravadists feel that in our era, only Gautama has reached buddhahood).

CHADO
The Way of Tea – the ritualistic aesthetic preparation and serving of tea to a few guests, involving special implements, vessels and flower arrangements, while pondering the four basic principles of harmony, respect, purity and tranquillity.

CH'AN
Chinese Buddhist school of meditation. See Zen.

CHORTEN
Tibetan term for stupa.

CONFUCIANISM
An essentially political and social set of teachings founded by the Chinese philosopher Confucius.

DALAI LAMA
Term of Mongolian origin meaning 'Ocean of wisdom', given to the spiritual and temporal leader of Tibet.

DHARMA
Buddhist doctrine that aids in the escape from the suffering of samsara, a law attributable to the historical Buddha, concerning the basic nature of phenomena.

DHYANA
Originally the name given to the First Meditation of Siddharta, the term was later adopted by an Indian Buddhist school of meditation. See Zen.

DOGEN
Buddhist monk and disciple of Eisai. He established the Soto sect of Zen Buddhism.

EISAI
Twelfth-century Buddhist monk who founded the Rinzai branch of Zen.

FIVE AGGREGATES
Human existence is a composite of the five aggregates (khandhas): corporeality or physical form, feelings or sensations, perception, mental formation (conditioned responses to one's experiences including intuition, determination and the idea of self) and consciousness. Clinging to the five aggregates leads to suffering.

FOUR NOBLE TRUTHS
These truths, preached by the historical Buddha, reveal the nature of suffering, its cause, its end and the path to its cessation.

GAUTAMA
Name of the historical Buddha.

GELUGPA
Fourth main school of Tibetan Buddhism, also known as 'the yellow hat sect', of which the current Dalai Lama is a member.

GOMCHENS
Tibetan religious laity.

HINAYANA
Lesser Vehicle, Southern school or Theravada (the School of the Ancients), a term coined by followers of the Mahayana to describe the path practised by those who adhere only to the earliest discourses as the word of the Buddha.

JAINISM
Ascetic religion, believing that those who free themselves from all fetters, through the practice of austerities and non-violence until they conquer jain (ignorance), will be delivered from the endless cycle of death and rebirth. The path of Jain liberation comprises right belief, right knowledge and right conduct. The prescriptions or rules of Jainism describe the way to achieve this liberation.

JATAKA
Stories or legends about the historical Buddha's previous lives.

KAGYUPA
The second main school of Tibetan Buddhism.

KARMA
Literally, actions or volitional activities under the cosmic law of cause and effect. Every physical or mental deed has a long-range consequence, as determined by the nature of the person's intention. There is positive, neutral and negative karma.

KARMAPA
High Official of Tibetan Buddhism and head of the Karma–Kagyupa school. Holds the power to transmit Enlightenment.

KHANDHAS
The five aggregates that lead to the suffering of mortals.

KOAN
A paradoxical anecdote or story used to bring Zen students to realization and help clarify their enlightenment.

KUSINAGARA
The place where the historical Buddha died. It is located in eastern Uttar Pradesh.

KYUDO
Zen Buddhist 'way of archery'.

LAMA
Honorific title given in Tibet to a 'master'. This spiritual teacher can be an ordained monk, but also a married Buddhist scholar. Lama is a translation of 'guru' ('master' in Sanskrit).

LAMAISM
Western term for Tibetan Buddhism.

LAMASERY
Tibetan Buddhist monastery.

LOTUS SUTRA
One of the most important Buddhist texts. The lotus symbolises purity.

LUMBINI
The birthplace of the historical Buddha, located in present-day Nepal.

MAHAVIRA
See Vardhamana.

MAHAYANA
Greater Vehicle, or Northern school, branch of Buddhism that builds on the original tradition (Theravada or Hinayana). In addition, it associates beings of compassion (bodhisattvas) with its teaching.

MAITREYA
Future buddha who will succeed the historical Buddha Siddharta Gautama and purify the world.

MANDALA
Pictorial diagram used in meditation. In the Vajrayana, it corresponds to a magical place, or a symbol of the universe, of buddhas and Tantric deities.

MANTRA
Sacred chant, often repeated, consisting of only one or two words or syllables, used in Mahayanist schools.

MARA
The personification of evil and temptation, who keeps mortals in their ignoble condition.

Glossary

MENDICANT
Wandering monk, depending on alms for a living.

MUDRAS
The hand gestures of the buddhas. There are over 130 of these.

NIRVANA
'Extinction'. This 'beyond suffering' is the ultimate liberation from samsara.

NOBLE EIGHTFOLD PATH
The 'Middle Way', which leads to the cessation of suffering. The eight categories that should be practised are Right Understanding, Right Intention, Right Speech, Right Action, Right Livelihood, Right Effort, Right Mindfulness, and Right Concentration.

NYINGMAPA
The first main school of Tibetan Buddhism.

PADMASAMBHAVA
Named Guru Rinpoche in Tibetan. Indian Tantric master who introduced Buddhism to the Himalayas and to Tibet.

PALI
Term meaning 'line of writing'. The canon of texts preserved by the Theravada school; ancient language of Southern India and Sri Lanka (Ceylon).

PANCHEN LAMA
High Tibetan Buddhist Official instituted by the fifth Dalai Lama and considered to be an emanation of the buddha Amitabha.

PARAMITA
The six perfections that aid in the Mahayanist quest for Enlightenment: generosity, patience, morality, diligence, meditation and transcendental wisdom.

PARINIRVANA
State of supreme deliverance from samsara, which marks the end of the cycle of rebirth.

PITAKA
See tipitaka.

POTALA
Tibetan palace of the Dalai Lamas.

RAHULA
Son of the historical Buddha.

RATNASAMBHAVA
One of the five meditation buddhas. The Jewel-Born One.

RINPOCHE
Term of respect, meaning 'precious one', given to the reincarnations of great Tibetan spiritual masters.

RINZAI
Branch of Zen Buddhism.

SAKYAPA
Third main school of Tibetan Buddhism.

SAKYAMUNI
'Sage of the Sakya lineage'. Surname given to Siddharta Gautama, the historical Buddha.

SAMANTABHADRA
Bodhisattva of All-Pervading Wisdom.

SAMSARA
Cycle of rebirth conditioned by karmic law.

SANGHA
Buddhist community comprising monks, nuns and laity.

SANSKRIT
Classical scholarly language of the Brahmins, sacred Indian texts and Mahayana Buddhism.

SATORI
Japanese term meaning the experience of spiritual Enlightenment in Zen Buddhism.

SENGAI
Japanese Zen monk, calligrapher and poet (1750–1837).

SHAMANISM
Archaic magico-religious phenomenon in which the shaman is the great master of ecstasy. A shaman may exhibit a particular magical specialty (such as control

over fire, wind or magical flight, or healing. Shamanism is characterised by its focus on an ecstatic trance state in which the soul of the shaman is believed to leave the body and ascend to the sky (heavens) or descend into the earth (underworld). The shaman makes use of spirit helpers, with whom he or she communicates, while all the time retaining control over his or her own consciousness.

SHINTO
Original shamanistic religion revering divine spirits.

SON
Korean Buddhist school of meditation. See Zen.

SONGTSEN GAMPO
Seventh-century Tibetan king who, with his two wives, helped to establish Buddhism in Tibet.

SOTO
School of Zen Buddhism.

STUPA (CHORTEN IN TIBETAN)
Buddhist edifice, originally a memorial to the Buddha.

SUDDHODANA
King or great chieftain of the Sakya tribe, father of the historical Buddha.

SUTRA
Transcription of the words that are attributed to the Buddha or his immediate disciples, including the Buddha's speeches and texts of the law.

TANTRA
Sanskrit word signifying 'thread' or 'weft' and now used to mean 'tract'. Esoteric text, transmitted,

according to the Vajrayana, by vision or inspiration.

TAOISM
Chinese cosmological doctrine that renounces worldly vanity and aspires to harmony and the contemplation of beauty.

TARA
Representation of feminine wisdom in buddhas. Tara means 'the liberator'.

TATHAGATA
Meaning those who have gone beyond, or those who have 'arrived', this refers to the six buddhas who are said to have preceded Siddharta Gautama, as well as to the Buddha himself.

THANGKA
Literally, 'something that is unrolled'. Painted, embroidered or woven banner that is unrolled during important ceremonies and is thought to possess good qualities.

THERAVADA
'Doctrine of the Ancients'. See Hinayana.

TIPITAKA
Name of the Buddhist canon written in Pali, comprising 'three baskets' of texts: the Buddha's speeches or texts of the law, monastic regulations and scholastic treatises.

TSCHECHUS
Signifies 'tenth' and celebrates the great feats that Padmasambhava would have performed on the tenth day.

TULKOU
In Tibetan Buddhism, the reincarnation of a being who is spiritually fulfilled (see Rinpoche).

UPANISHADISM
Early Hindu religion involving the study of the Upanishads, founded as a result of meditations on many of the themes found in Vedic texts.

UPANISHADS
The principal texts of the Hindu religion, compiled in the period 800–500 BC. Each upanishad is the last part of a Veda (sacred Hindu scripture) and gives strict injunctions regarding ethics, rituals and forms of meditation. Upanishads are exclusively dedicated to philosophical discussions on how to obtain the real wisdom or real enlightenment.

VAIROCANA
One of the meditation buddhas. The Radiating One.

VAJRAYANA
Diamond Vehicle or Tantrism. Branch of Buddhism that emphasises meditative practices and initiation by a spiritual master.

VARDHAMANA
The founder of Jainism. He is also known as Mahavira.

VEDA
Religious text, made up of thousands of hymns and sacred and poetic phrases, predating Brahminism and Buddhism.

VEDISM
A pre-Brahmin school of Indian religious thought, based on a body of sacred texts.

VEHICLE
Term designating the different branches of Buddhism. There are three: the Lesser Vehicle ('Hinayana'), the Greater Vehicle ('Mahayana') and the Diamond Vehicle ('Vajrayana'). 'Yana' means 'Vehicle'.

VINAYA
'Discipline'. Rules of life for monks and nuns.

VOIDNESS
State of 'great emptiness'. Essential Buddhist term. All phenomena, according to Buddhists, are void of their own existence. They are but a set of elements.

YASODHARA
Princess and wife of the historical Buddha.

ZAZEN
Traditional Zen meditation technique, carried out seated in the lotus position or cross-legged, in order to reach a state of voidness. It is practised by the Soto sect.

ZEN
Mahayana Buddhist school of meditation, of Indian origin (dhyana), which developed in China (Ch'an) and then in Korea (Son), before reaching Japan. Contemplation and intuitive comprehension are the foundation of this tradition, which is tied to nature and its beauty.

Table of contents

Fact ⟫ 2–12
Fun facts and quick quotes

Discover ⟫ 13–38

Look ⟫ 39–56
The treasures of the temples of Nara and Kyoto in Japan

In Practice ⟫ 57–86

Find Out » 87–125

Credits

P. 14, Photothèque Hachette – **P. 16**, Musée Guimet, Paris - Artephot/Lavaud – **P. 19**, Artephot/Hanz Hinz – **P. 20**, Sarnath Museum - Artephot/R. Roland – **P. 23**, Musée Guimet, Paris - Artephot/Lavaud – **P. 24**, Musée Guimet, Paris - Artephot/G. Mandel – **P. 27** Musée Guimet, Paris - Artephot/Lavaud – **P. 28–29**, Sarnath Museum/ M. Pietri – **P. 31**, Artephot/J. Lavaud – **P. 32**, Musée Guimet, Paris, photo RMN/Thierry Ollivier – **P. 35**, R. Burri/Magnum photos – **P. 36**, Musée d'Orsay - Artephot/R. Jourdain – **P. 40–56** : Artephot/K. Ogawa – **P. 58–86**, MISS graphics – **P. 63**, Hiuang-Tsang, negative Artephot/R. Percheron – **P. 64-65**, Musée Guimet, RMN negative/ Richard Lambert – **P. 66**, negative (top left) C. Boisvieux ; negatives (top right and bottom) J.-L. Nou – **P. 67**, negative J.-L. Nou – **P. 72**, negative Matthieu Ricard/Agence Vu – **P. 74**, Musée Guimet/negative RMN - Arnaudet – **P. 76 –77**, negatives Matthieu Ricard/Agence Vu – **P. 80-81**, negatives G. Nencioli/Phare International – **P. 82**, negative Artephot/Nimatallah – **P. 83**, negatives (top and bottom) T. Hopker/Magnum – **P. 84**, negative (top) V. Pcholkin/Stock Image; negative (bottom) Artephot/M. Pietri – **P. 85**, negative (top) Artephot/Ogawa ; negative (bottom) Stock Image – **P. 88–125**, illustrations Philippe Andrieu – **P. 97**, negative The Newark Museum/Art Ressource, NY – **P. 99**, negative Arturo Patten / Opale – **P. 105**, Museum of History of Religion, Ulan Bator, Mongolia – **P. 106**, drawing of workshop Henri and Bruno Gaudin/Ministère de la Culture et de la Communication (France), for the Musée Guimet – **P. 113**, cliché Artephot/Takase – **P. 117**, negative Cristophe L.

Acknowledgements

The author would like to thank Jean-Paul Ribes and Junko Saito for their invaluable advice, as well as Léo Diamand for his friendly support. He wishes great wisdom upon Philippe Andrieu, the 'mad illustrator' of the last pages of this book.

IMEI 448835-41-967963-5